When God Speaks
through You

When God Speaks through You

How Faith Convictions Shape Preaching and Mission

Craig A. Satterlee

THE
ALBAN
INSTITUTE

Herndon, Virginia
www.alban.org

The Alban Institute
2121 Cooperative Way, Suite 100
Herndon, VA 20171

Scripture quotations, unless otherwise noted, are from the New Revised Standard Version of the Bible, © 1989, Division of Christian Education of the National Council of Churches of Christ in the United States of America, and are used by permission.

Cover design by Tobias Becker.

Library of Congress Cataloging-in-Publication Data

Satterlee, Craig Alan, 1959-
  When God speaks through you : how faith convictions shape preaching and mission / Craig A. Satterlee.
    p. cm. -- (The vital worship, healthy congregations series)
  Includes bibliographical references.
  ISBN-13: 978-1-56699-353-1
  1. Preaching. I. Title.
  BV4211.3.S34 2007
  251—dc22
                                                    2007035172

    12   11   10   09   08   VG   1   2   3   4   5

For Graduates, Participants, and Faculty of the
ACTS Doctor of Ministry in Preaching Program,
particularly my colleagues
John A. Dally
W. Dow Edgerton
J. Frederick Holper
Carol M. Norén
Michael Shelley
Danna E. Gobel

Contents

Editor's Foreword

Healthy Congregations

Christianity is a "first-person plural" religion, where communal worship, service, fellowship, and learning are indispensable for grounding and forming individual faith. The strength of Christianity in North America depends on the presence of healthy, spiritually nourishing, well-functioning congregations. Congregations are the cradle of Christian faith, the communities in which children of all ages are supported, encouraged, and formed for lives of service. Congregations are the habitat in which the practices of the Christian life can flourish.

As living organisms, congregations are by definition in a constant state of change. Whether the changes are in membership, pastoral leadership, lay leadership, the needs of the community, or the broader culture, a crucial mark of healthy congregations is their ability to deal creatively and positively with change. The fast pace of change in contemporary culture, with its bias toward, not against, change only makes the challenge of negotiating change all the more pressing for congregations.

Vital Worship

At the center of many discussions about change in churches today is the topic of worship. This is not surprising, for worship is at the center of congregational life. To "go to church" means, for most members of congregations, "to go to worship." In *How Do We*

Worship?, Mark Chaves begins his analysis with the simple assertion, "Worship is the most central and public activity engaged
in by American religious congregations" (Alban Institute, 1999,
p. 1). Worship styles are one of the most significant reasons that
people choose to join a given congregation. Correspondingly, they
are central to the identity of most congregations.

Worship is also central on a much deeper level. Worship is the
locus of what several Christian traditions identify as the nourishing center of congregational life: preaching, common prayer, and
the celebration of ordinances or sacraments. Significantly, what
many traditions elevate to the status of "the means of grace" or
even the "marks of the church" are essentially liturgical actions.
Worship is central, most significantly, for theological reasons.
Worship both reflects and shapes a community's faith. It expresses
a congregation's view of God and enacts a congregation's relationship with God and each other.

We can identify several specific factors that contribute to spiritually vital worship and thereby strengthen congregational life.

- Congregations, and the leaders that serve them, need a
  shared vision for worship that is grounded in more than
  personal aesthetic tastes. This vision must draw on the
  deep theological resources of Scripture, the Christian tradition, and the unique history of the congregation.
- Congregational worship should be integrated with the
  whole life of the congregation. It can serve as the "source
  and summit" from which all the practices of the Christian life flow. Worship both reflects and shapes the life of
  the church in education, pastoral care, community service,
  fellowship, justice, hospitality, and every other aspect of
  church life.
- The best worship practices feature not only good worship
  "content," such as discerning sermons, honest prayers,
  creative artistic contributions, celebrative and meaningful
  rituals for baptism and the Lord's Supper. They also arise
  of out of good process, involving meaningful contributions
  from participants, thoughtful leadership, honest evaluation, and healthy communication among leaders.

Vital Worship, Healthy Congregations Series

The Vital Worship, Healthy Congregations Series is designed to reflect the kind of vibrant, creative energy and patient reflection that will promote worship that is both relevant and profound. It is designed to invite congregations to rediscover a common vision for worship, to sense how worship is related to all aspects of congregational life, and to imagine better ways of preparing both better "content" and better "process" related to the worship life of their own congregations.

It is important to note that strengthening congregational life through worship renewal is a delicate and challenging task precisely because of the uniqueness of each congregation. This book series is not designed to represent a single denomination, Christian tradition, or type of congregation. Nor is it designed to serve as arbiter of theological disputes about worship. Books in the series will note the significance of theological claims about worship, but they may, in fact, represent quite different theological visions from each other, or from our work at the Calvin Institute of Christian Worship. That is, the series is designed to call attention to instructive examples of congregational life and to explore these examples in ways that allow readers in very different communities to compare and contrast these examples with their own practice. The models described in any given book may for some readers be instructive as examples to follow. For others, a given example may remind them of something they are already doing well, or something they will choose not to follow because of theological commitments or community history.

In *When God Speaks through You: How Faith Convictions Shape Preaching and Mission,* Craig Satterlee encourages us to resist thinking of the sermon as the act of a single person, but rather as a communal action. Sermons should ideally be as communal an act as congregational singing. The lynchpin to this new understanding is the act of listening. Preachers need to cultivate a much more intentional way of listening to worshipers, and worshipers need to cultivate a deeper mode of listening to preachers. When active listening is practiced pervasively, the result is a congregational

culture of active reception for the gift of God's word, word that
promises to both comfort and convict not just individuals, but entire communities. As you read and study this book, I encourage
you think especially about the culture of preaching and listening
over time. No single sermon can achieve every purpose or connect
with every type of person. But a great deal can be accomplished
over time to draw in the voices, communication styles, and unique
insights of both the astonishing diversity of biblical voices and the
astonishing diversity of voices in our congregations.

By promoting encounters with instructive examples from various parts of the body of Christ, we pray that these volumes will
help leaders make good judgments about worship in their congregations and that, by the power of God's Spirit, these congregations
will flourish.

John D. Witvliet
Calvin Institute for Christian Worship

Foreword

When I hear someone is writing a book, sooner or later I ask what it is about. Every author can tell you what the topic is. But what is it really about? Often one hears stumbling and stuttering, signals that even by the writing stage an author has not formulated the theme and approach and cannot articulate it.

I got to know Craig Satterlee rather casually, but whenever I asked him a question about his projects, I got clear answers. One day we agreed to meet to discuss his next book. Nothing was yet on paper. Without giving him time to get settled in his chair I asked him: "Exactly, what is your book going to be about? What do you hope to achieve through it? How will it be different from other books in its field?" He was ready. He didn't ask for a research grant, a sabbatical, or even a day to think it over

William James wrote that every good author has a "commanding vision," something that draws in and compels the reader to follow as the argument or plot develops. Professor Satterlee did have in mind what preaching meant for him and what he hoped to bring out of others who preach or who listen to homilies and sermons. More important, through years of teaching, he had given good thought to what the gospel of Jesus Christ means or can mean to those who preach and to those who listen to homilies and sermons.

What I found valuable in his condensation of the plot and approach is that he had a focus on the audience, the hearers, which in Christian settings means the congregation. In many books for preachers and hearers, one can infer that a congregation is out there, but the whole accent is on the experience, make-up, training, research, intention, and delivery of the preacher. Not here.

I've long been looking for the accent on the hearer in many books of rhetoric. In Aristotle's world, three things especially matter. First, the *ethos* or character of the speaker. It is hard to hear the gospel from a moral scandalizer, but one is ready to hear from someone who is exemplary. Third is the *logos*, which in preaching is the gospel. Between them is the *pathos*, which we find in words like "sympathy" and "empathy," but which we can translate as the situation of the congregation or audience or hearers. Satterlee is a *pathos* writer, who never forgets *ethos* or *logos*.

We have many histories of preaching to and almost none of hearing congregations. Most professional preachers have to depend on the findings, admittedly meager, offered them by ethnographers, but the best of them get their understandings because they converse well, hear well, respect and love people, and take seriously what they reveal about themselves. Satterlee does this, and the result is patent in this book.

When God Speaks Through You is rich in detail. God evidently has much to speak and say through "you," you make up "all sorts and conditions" of the human experience. This book can only give leads and help one acquire tools for accession to "what" God speaks through you. Thanks to little question-and-answer sessions for hearers and speakers at the end of the chapters, one acquires a kind of do-it-yourself kit for enlarging the scope of what might be said, and thus heard.

After Craig Satterlee spun out what his book would be about on the spot that day we parted. During the year that followed I chanced to do some interim-emergency-part-time-ad hoc-adjunct-joint teaching at the Lutheran School of Theology at Chicago, the school where Satterlee teaches.

Not long after my stint I received this manuscript from him, and I got to follow through with pleasurable reading of a clear, coherent book whose author has a "commanding vision"—of the gospel for our day.

Martin E. Marty
Fairfax M. Cone Distinguished Service
Professor Emeritus, University of Chicago

Preface

A book takes on a life all its own. I never anticipated that my first book for the Vital Worship, Healthy Congregations Series, *When God Speaks through Change: Preaching in Times of Congregational Transition,*[1] which I intended for preachers, would find an audience among people in the pew. Nor did I anticipate that churchgoers would invite me into their congregations and approach me at conferences to ask, "How about a book for us?" When I inquired about what they had in mind, people often reported that they agree with me that what I call "holy and active listening," listening openly and attentively to one another with the expectation that God will speak in and through the conversation, is essential to preaching and leading a congregation through transition.[2] However, they added, listening is very difficult when members of a congregation sit down to talk about an issue that causes discomfort, tension, and even division within the congregation. Because congregational members are not practiced in this kind of listening, the issue they need to discuss frequently stalls their conversation. "Give us something to get the conversation started. Give us a tool to help us talk with each other and to talk with our pastor," they said. People also reported that, in reading and discussing *When God Speaks through Change* with members of their congregation, they discovered they like to talk about preaching.

This is no surprise to me. Pastors who participate in the Doctor of Ministry in Preaching Program of the Association of Chicago Theological Schools (ACTS), of which I am privileged to serve as dean, overwhelmingly report that their work with a group of parishioners who provide input and feedback on sermons and discuss preaching with the pastor is the most rewarding, even transforming, part of the program. They attest that talking about preaching frequently results in spiritual growth, renewal, deeper appreciation for difference, new perspective, and motivation not only for the preacher but also for the members of the parish group and, through them, the congregation.

A Conversation Starter

I offer this book to those who listen to sermons and to their preachers as a tool, an icebreaker, a conversation starter, a way of priming the pump of congregational conversation so that holy and active listening can occur. This book is about preaching and some of the faith convictions that individuals who come to church bring with them to the Sunday sermon. I hope that reading this book together and discussing it will help faith communities—both preachers and people in the pew—discover their expectations of and reactions to preaching. These conversations can certainly revitalize the congregation's preaching ministry, as the preacher knows a little better what people listen for and as parishioners understand a little better what the preacher hopes to accomplish in the Sunday sermon. I believe that when individuals and faith communities talk about preaching they will identify, clarify, and articulate their convictions about the Christian faith and can learn to share them in a nonthreatening manner. In this way, discussing sermons and preaching can generate a broader conversation about how people's convictions about the Christian faith shape both their lives and the congregation's worship, life together, and mission. Such conversations can better prepare congregations to address the challenges they face in a healthy and constructive manner.

This book does not eliminate differences; it is not a practical, how-to guide for getting rid of the tension that Christians inevitably experience as they seek to allow God's saving activity in Jesus Christ to form and direct their lives. Too often churchgoers try to eliminate tension, both in church and in their ordinary lives, by pronouncing absolute truths and prescriptive actions. These attempts often accomplish nothing more than creating "insiders" and "outsiders." Rather than eliminating tension, this book invites Christians to embrace tension as an opportunity to discern how and where the Spirit is leading and as an opportunity to discover points of concord, consensus, and conflict among members of their congregations. In this spirit, rather than providing a single perspective with which people can agree or disagree, my approach is (1) to articulate convictions that preachers and congregants bring to preaching and (2) to provide a space, an arena in congregational life in which conversation can take place. I ask some questions about sermons and provide some answers. Both the questions and answers grow out of my reflections on countless conversations with churchgoers—both preachers and people in the pew—about what they believe about, hope for, and expect from preaching and how these convictions shape their lives and their congregations.

The questions I ask are not an exhaustive list. None of the answers I offer is right or wrong, and that is the point. Rather than making choices, this book invites you to locate yourself among various points of view or to add a perspective that I have not identified. By using this book to discuss preaching, you will find that people in your congregation hold many different convictions about what the sermon is and ought to do. If people in the same congregation have different perspectives on something as safe and central as the Sunday sermon, they should not be surprised that they hold different views on other, perhaps more difficult issues. Discussing and listening to their different perspectives on preaching will help churchgoers learn to talk together about other issues they face.

For this process to work, pastor and parishioners must journey together as co-learners. Participants in the process must be clear that the topic of conversation is preaching and not the preacher. Discussing sermons makes every preacher feel vulnerable at some level because the focus is on people's expectations of and convictions about preaching. For their part, preachers may need to be patient with their conversation partners, including this book, whose answers might not be as forthright, developed, and definitive as their own. I deliberately approach questions and answers about preaching in different ways, in the hope that one of those ways will connect with everyone in the conversation; therefore, this book may sometimes seem repetitive. Preachers may also need to fight the temptation to "correct" others' answers and claim a teaching moment. As a Lutheran pastor, I know that this is how I often respond when parishioners talk in ways that sound to me a little too much like works righteousness. Finally, if you are looking for a revolutionary new approach that will drastically improve either your own preaching or that of your pastor, you will not find one here, because that is not why I wrote this book.

While you who use this book may have different convictions, I encourage you to also hold two things in common or the conversation will remain theoretical and academic. First, I encourage you to agree that diverse perspectives are inherent to the church and that preaching both surfaces and responds to this diversity. I address this topic in the introduction. Second, I encourage you who use this book to recognize that preaching alone cannot maintain a lively faith for either a Christian or a congregation. Preaching is part of a congregation's ministry, and the sermon is part of the worship service. Congregations need more than the bold, faithful leadership that comes from excellent preaching; they need gospel-centered leadership in every aspect of congregational life. As in so many areas of individual faith and common life, both *worship* and *leadership* are subjects that Christians and congregations have many different convictions about. Defining *leadership* and *worship* is a challenging task. Therefore, I devote chapters 1 and 2 to these topics and their relationship to preaching. In chapter 1, I ask, "Is preaching leadership?" I consider how current understandings of leadership relate to Jesus's preaching and the preaching of the church. In chapter 2 I ask, "How does the sermon fit into the worship service?" I describe characteristics that aid congregations in considering their worship and suggest that we can describe the relationship of worship and mission as a mountain, a plain, and a river. I then turn to the convictions that people bring to the Sunday sermon.

People bring many convictions to the Sunday sermon. Some assumptions can be clarified and classified according to people's generational type, gender, cultural background, learning style, social location, and political persuasion.[3] While sermons expose many kinds of assumptions, I find that responding to sermons and discussing preaching reveal how people appropriate the Christian faith and relate it to their daily lives. The experiences, perspectives, and beliefs that shape how people listen to (or preach) the sermon and relate it to their lives also lead them to hold convictions about the Christian faith. As I said, these Christian convictions are not consistent among members of a congregation, let alone in the mind of an individual member or even the preacher. In fact, the center of gravity or essence of people's individual and corporate faith, as well as a congregation's preaching, varies from time to time and place to place.

Christians certainly express their faith convictions differently; however, I find that these convictions cluster around six topics: (1) the purpose of preaching, (2) the essence of faith, (3) Christian living, (4) Christian community, (5) the church's mission, and (6) the future. In chapters 3 through 8, I invite groups within congregations to discuss their convictions about these topics, using preaching and sermons to facilitate the conversation. In the epilogue, I offer general reflections on how discussing these convictions relates to worship and leadership. Also, because I suspect that this conversation will lead to further conversations about sermons and preaching, I include three approaches for discussing sermons and preaching that have been provided by preachers, congregations, and teachers of preaching.

Chapters 3 through 5 help churchgoers and pastors consider their faith. In chapter 3, I invite you to name what you consider to be the purpose of preaching. I ask, "What is a sermon?" How people understand a sermon's purpose reveals the question or the concern they bring to preaching and what they hope to get from the sermon, as well as what they expect the sermon to do or to accomplish. Naming the purpose of preaching is a way to describe their reason or motivation for connecting the Christian faith and their lives. Is it fear, hope, guidance, or direction? In chapter 4, I ask, "How do you listen to sermons?" Though most churchgoers hear sermons through their ears, people tend to listen to sermons using a filter such as head or heart. By discovering how you and others in the congregation listen to sermons, you can discover where your faith lives and what your faith is like. You identify the means you and others use to connect the Christian faith and your lives. For some, it is the intellect; for others, emotion. Still others connect faith and action. Regarding Christian living, the topic of chapter 5, I ask, "How do you hope preaching will influence your daily life?" Christians, both preachers and people who listen to sermons, expect preaching to connect with daily life in different ways; their expectations influence both the way they respond to sermons and the way they live as disciples.

Chapters 6 through 8 help you and others in your congregation consider how you relate to your faith community. To explore your understanding of Christian community, the topic of chapter 6, I ask both preachers and listeners, "How do you engage the congregation during preaching?" For most people, church is a place. But what kind of place? The place you describe reveals how you relate to other members of the congregation. Chapter 7 is concerned with the church's mission. I ask, "Through preaching, what is the most important thing God calls your congregation to do?" The church's mission is described in several ways that draw from Scripture. Different scriptural commissions are certainly variations on a common theme. Christians and congregations, as they seek to connect their congregation with God's work of salvation, resonate with some variations more than others. In chapter 8, I ask, "How does preaching help people face the future?" The answer depends on how people understand the future; how Christians understand the future reveals what they expect from God. The epilogue includes both general reflections on the conversation and suggestions to help pastors and congregations continue to converse about sermons and preaching.

To model the conversation between preachers and listeners that I seek to facilitate, I attempt to give equal voice to hearers and preachers as I present each subject. As the chapter descriptions indicate, I begin each chapter with a question. I then offer possible responses to help people consider their convictions. The faith convictions I describe are conversation starters and not definitive answers to the questions I pose. In fact, the answer that best describes a particular Christian or congregation may be missing from this book. As you read and discuss each chapter, you might ask:

- Which response is most true for me?
- How would I tailor or modify that response to make it fit me better?
- What additional response would I add?

In each chapter, you will see a graphic that summarizes that chapter's central question and the various perspectives from which it is addressed. I chose to use these graphics rather than lists, because lists sometimes suggest (or are interpreted to suggest) hierarchical relationships among the elements, which can be misleading. First Corinthians reminds us that to categorize Christians and congregations, or to rank them from lesser to greater or lower to higher, is contrary to the gospel. Therefore, the graphics in this book are intended simply to convey, "Here are some perspectives on this question." In providing different perspectives as answers to questions about preaching, my aim is to help faith communities grow as the body of Christ by better understanding individual members. I present various perspectives that address the question, but you and other discussants might also want to use the graphic to help you explore relationships among the perspectives. For example:

- Circle or draw connecting lines between perspectives that are similar in some way. Add a label that identifies how they are similar.
- Draw a dotted circle around or a line between perspectives you think are most clearly dissimilar. Label your circle or line.
- Write your name next to the perspective most like your own.
- Mark an X next to the perspective least like your own.
- Put a question mark next to the perspective you would most like to explore.
- Write your congregation's name next to the perspectives you think are most strongly held by members of your congregation as a whole.

- Write the names of specific groups within your congregation next to the perspectives they seem to hold.
- Think about the people who regularly preach in your congregation. Write their names next to the appropriate perspective.
- Add branches to perspectives you think could be divided into subtopics. Label each branch.
- Add perspectives you think are missing.
- Come up with your own ideas!

To facilitate discussion, I also suggest as shorthand labels biblical images or verses that rely particularly on Jesus's sermons as recorded in the Gospels. The purpose of these biblical examples is to scripturally ground and orient the convictions that these responses represent and not to provide an extensive commentary on the Bible. While this book is not itself an in-depth Bible study, ideally it invites preachers and congregants to celebrate, renew, or undertake Bible study together. I provide Scripture citations not to "proof text," but to make it easier for groups to open their Bibles together. Since all the convictions have biblical examples and are scripturally warranted, preachers and hearers are freed from deciding between right and wrong. Instead, they can discover the convictions represented in their faith communities and how these convictions impact preaching—and, through preaching, congregational life.

Drawing on Jesus's preaching is different from responding to sermons we hear in church. First, we possess neither a DVD of Jesus preaching nor transcripts of Jesus's sermons, and a gap of perhaps 30 years exists between Jesus's death and resurrection and the creation of any written record about him. Nevertheless, what Jesus said and did was not lost; Jesus's preaching was kept alive orally by wandering Christian preachers and by followers of Christ, who "devoted themselves to the apostles' teaching and fellowship, to the breaking of bread and the prayers."[4] In time, the Gospel writers preserved recollections of Jesus's sermons, which provide both the crystallization of Jesus's preaching and clues to what the Gospel writers found memorable or important. These sermon recollections are summarized in Figure P.1.

Figure P.I. Scriptural Recollections of Jesus's Sermons

	Matthew	Mark	Luke	John
Sermon on the Mount	5:1-7:29			
Sermon to the Disciples	5:1-7:29	6:6-13	10:1-16	4:31-38
Sermon of the Parables	9:35-10:42			
Sermon in the Temple	13:1-52	11:17-12:44		
Sermon on Last Things	21:23-23:39			
Sermon at Nazareth	24:1-25:46		4:17-20	
Discourse on the Bread of Life				6:26-59

Second, Jesus's preaching is somewhat different from the preaching of the church. For example, some argue that Jesus preached about the reign of God while the church preaches about Jesus. Yet, while Jesus is God's unconditional love and the church preaches God's unconditional love in Christ, Jesus and the church proclaim the same gospel. Moreover, some argue that, while both Jesus's preaching and the preaching of the apostles were often accompanied by signs, similar signs are frequently either lacking or suspect in the preaching of the church. Or are they? While reports of God's saving acts may not be as concise and unambiguous as they appear in the Gospels, when we listen to God's people, we discover that signs of God's presence, love, and power continue in the lives of contemporary Christians and congregations. Finally, some argue that the context in which Jesus preached is very different from our own. For example, while those who traveled with Jesus heard him preach consistently, Jesus's preaching was more itinerant than much of the church's preaching. Yet, some scholars assert that circumstances today are more like that of Jesus and the apostles than any period in Christian history. For example, itinerant preaching continues, except today the listeners rather than the preacher come and go. Acknowledging these differences and considering their significance aids useful reflection on Jesus's preaching and its implications for the preaching of the church. Following the discussion of each answer, each chapter concludes with questions for discussion.

As I wrote this book, I was very aware of the groups in congregations that will use it to discuss preaching and their faith. I pray that you experience God speaking in and through your conversation.

Acknowledgments

This book took shape one afternoon at the round table in Martin E. Marty's studio near Chicago. "Marty" is one of the most prominent interpreters of religion and culture today. I admire Marty most for his gracious manner, probing questions, clarifying comments, and wise reflections, which pulled the book out of me that afternoon. The outline, and subsequently the manuscript, was refined and improved by my editor and friend, Beth Gaede, who has an uncanny ability to make whatever I write better. Parish pastors, in particular Timothy V. Olson and Melinda J. Wagner, carefully read chapter drafts and generously offered their own synthesis and reflection. This book is a bit like an iceberg. Plenty of scholarship, particularly homiletic theory, hides beneath the surface. While you may never see it, it shapes this book nonetheless. So I gratefully acknowledge my debt to my colleagues in the Academy of Homiletics. I also thank the Lutheran School of Theology at Chicago for granting me a sabbatical leave to write this book. Andrea Lee gave the book its final polish.

In chapter 4, I talk about the places where a person's faith makes its home. My faith makes its home in congregations at worship, particularly when I am privileged to preach and administer the sacraments. Three Lutheran congregations in Chicagoland—Grace in River Forest, Immanuel in Evanston, and St. Andrew in Glenwood—blessed me with that privilege for extended periods during my sabbatical, and I thank those saints. My faith also makes its home in holy places where I experience God's presence—Platte Lake in Michigan; Myrtle Beach, South Carolina; the University of Notre Dame; Walt Disney World; as well as my home in Hyde Park. Thanks to all who made it possible for me to spend time writing in each of these holy places.

My student assistant, Stephanie Lord, ran the interference necessary to ensure that my time away was a sabbath of rest, reflection, and writing. Steph also assisted with research, particularly the approaches to conversation included in the epilogue, and greatly improved the manuscript by her careful reading of drafts, reflections, and suggestions.

My daughter, Chelsey, who remains convinced that a better book would be *The Angry Flock: Why Do We Have to Change?* (complete with an image of sheep pummeling their shepherd), designed all the graphics in this book. My wife, Cathy, graced me with a sabbatical from the alarm clock, the calendar, and household chores (as if I actually do a lot around the house!). Cathy encouraged me to write when I needed to write, to rest when I needed to rest, and, above all, to enjoy what I was doing.

As you read this book, you will come to know Audrey, Brian, Connie, Drew, Eleanor, Fred, Lisa, Gail, and Pastor Mark. I am grateful to these fictional characters for engaging conversation about preaching and to the real-life characters, who contributed their names (though not their personalities), for our ongoing conversation about faith and life. The fictional characters you meet in this book represent preachers and parishioners who talk together about preaching and have graciously invited me to listen in. Each summer about a hundred preachers and twenty preaching professors come together in Chicago for the residency of the ACTS Doctor of Ministry in Preaching Program—three weeks devoted to preaching and talking about preaching. During the "school year," those pastors meet with a group of parishioners to consider preaching. Their insights, affirmations, and corrections enrich my teaching and scholarship, as well as my preaching. Reports of the transformation in individual and communal lives that results from their conversations about preaching inspire me. I thank God for congregations, pastors, and teachers convinced of the power of preaching and committed to the proclamation of the gospel. I am especially grateful for those colleagues with whom I share responsibility for overseeing the program and who bring such grace and support to my vocation. With joy and thanksgiving, I dedicate this book to the community that is the ACTS Doctor of Ministry in Preaching Program, especially my friends John, Dow, Fred, Carol, Mike, and Danna.

Introduction

Is homosexuality a sin? What is the Christian response to war? Is stem-cell research a gift from God? Today Christians and congregations divide on issues ranging from what constitutes appropriate Christian behavior to how to use the congregation's financial resources. People of faith and goodwill hold different perspectives on the relationship between religion and science and the way Christianity fits in the culture. These differences become obvious when issues of faith and daily life are discussed from the pulpit. Perhaps this is why some preachers cower and some parishioners squirm when the Spirit nudges a sermon to address issues like sex, money, power, and politics. Even when they flow directly from the Scripture that was read in worship, sermons on abortion, divorce, capital punishment, and sometimes supposedly safe subjects, such as God's love for *all* people, reveal that Christians regularly bring their own convictions to the sermon. This is true not only for preachers but also for all the baptized.

Sometimes, instead of the sermon's subject or content revealing our different convictions, the theological axioms at work in the sermon may disclose that what we hold to be true is not held to be true by everyone. For example, some Christians assume that God is omnipotent and are startled when a sermon addresses a difficult situation from the perspective that God is not all-powerful. Others assume that politics has no place in the pulpit, and they may be offended by preachers who bring the faith into the public square and the public square into the pulpit. Sometimes sermons help us name convictions that we hold, which we may never have put into words. We may think, "That sermon makes it sound like the Bible might not be literally true. I don't believe that." Or, "I don't care what people are asking for. I am not going to preach about who is going to hell." The way a sermon is crafted may reveal our convictions. What kinds of sermon illustrations are and are not acceptable? Should preachers tell stories about themselves or members of the congregation? How a sermon is delivered can even reveal what we hold to be true, acceptable, or appropriate. For example, what should (and shouldn't) a minister wear to preach? Once parishioners presented me with a new pair of shoes they described as "more befitting the pulpit."

Sometimes our convictions are revealed by the needs we bring to a sermon, rather than the sermon itself, and by how well a sermon meets those needs. We may need to know what a particular passage of Scripture means or who God is and what God expects of us. To meet these needs, we want sermons that are informational. When we need to feel God's love and be assured of God's goodwill and care, sermons should touch our hearts. We may need a sermon to equip us to talk about Jesus to our children or to respond to a friend in crisis. We may need a sermon to tell us how God is involved in what is happening in the world. We may not know our needs as we listen to a sermon. Pastor Roger Van Harn observes that we do not come to a sermon with our needs neatly packaged so that we can open them and have them solved one by one as we listen. "We come with a confusion of needs: needs we want to hide, needs that cry out to be met, needs that can wait, and needs we do not even know. We need to be addressed in our needs, and we cannot even understand them without the grace that brings the remedy."[1]

Liturgical historian James F. White observes that "what one brings to church determines in large measure what one experiences there."[2] Sometimes we assume that the convictions we bring to the Sunday sermon are universally true for all Christians and the church. When we discover that the preacher or other members of the congregation hold convictions different from our own, struggles and divisions may surface; as in many extended families, discussing certain issues and working together to resolve them might become difficult. Yet, as long as our convictions remain unspoken and undefined, Christians and congregations cannot address difficult issues, in part, because we talk past one another. Preachers and parishioners talk past each other, as do individuals and groups within congregations. The struggles that result may

even splinter congregations, should Christians conclude that anyone who does not share their convictions lacks faith or is not committed to Christ.

Christians have always held different convictions about their
faith. As the writer of Ecclesiastes reminds us, "there is nothing
new under the sun."[3] In fact, biblical scholars and church histo-
rians see parallels between the divisions of the earliest Christian
communities and those of our own time, including "struggles between churches over a diversity of traditions and struggles within
an individual church over interpretations of the same tradition."[4]
The book of Acts demonstrates that diversity, disagreement, and
even division characterized the church of the apostles. While Acts
2 describes life among the believers in the period after Pentecost as idyllic, when "all who believed were together and had all
things in common,"[5] read on and you will find that people's differing convictions about following Christ caused controversy and
conflict within the church. Peter's ministry to Gentiles in Cae-
sarea led the believers and apostles in Judea to criticize him for
going to the uncircumcised and eating with them. The council at
Jerusalem was convened after Paul and Barnabas "had no small
dissension and debate" with believers from Judea who taught that
to be saved people had to be circumcised. Away from Jerusalem,
Paul and Barnabas's disagreement over John Mark's participation
in their ministry became so sharp that Paul and Barnabas parted
company.[6] Throughout Christian history, from Acts to our own
day, circumstances created a plurality of Christian perspectives,
which often resulted in conflict. Sometimes the church resolved
conflict by arriving at a consensus. The church resolved other
conflicts by establishing canon and creeds. Still other conflicts
resulted in schism and reformation. Though Christians responded in different ways, diverse convictions and even conflict about
believing in and following Christ have always characterized the
church.

Our Postmodern Context

Today many congregations and their pastors understand the diversity and division that characterize the contemporary church as

a consequence of the postmodern ethos of the late twentieth and early twenty-first century. In *The Postmodern Parish*, Jim Kitchens writes, "By postmodernism, we mean that people lack the kind of faith in science they had a generation ago, look more to unmediated experience than to rational thought to give meaning to their lives, and doubt that one single metanarrative can explain the world."[7] Postmodernity is complicated because most people both embrace and resist it. Ronald J. Allen, Professor of Preaching and New Testament at Christian Theological Seminary in Indianapolis, explains postmodernism using four challenges to the notion that knowledge is absolute and experience universal.[8]

First, the postmodern spirit respects pluralism and honors the unique experience and integrity of individuals and faith communities. Today many Christians agree both that the Bible is God's word and that Christians can read the same passage of Scripture and interpret it differently. For example, what does John 13:14 mean? Jesus said, "So if I, your Lord and Teacher, have washed your feet, you also ought to wash one another's feet." Should washing one another's feet be part of our Christian practice or was Jesus speaking metaphorically? Is Jesus addressing us or is Jesus only speaking to the first disciples? We may be able to discuss this passage objectively and dispassionately. However, when their own interpretations, core beliefs, identity, and worldview are threatened by how others interpret Scripture, most Christians dismiss those interpretations as incorrect.

Second, postmoderns are aware that social location (one's race, class, gender, sexual orientation, religion, and physical ability) shapes our perceptions of reality. In Exodus, for example, Moses and the people sing, "Pharaoh's chariots and his army [God] cast into the sea; his picked officers were sunk in the Red Sea. The floods covered them; they went down into the depths like a stone."[9] Postmoderns recognize that the wife of a drowned Egyptian officer would certainly experience the parting of the Red Sea differently than Moses and Israel and would sing a different song, probably a funeral hymn. Postmoderns acknowledge that both songs are true, depending on one's social location. Yet we resist other interpretations when another's song drowns out or negates the song we are singing.

Third, a postmodern approach challenges and deconstructs (or makes operating assumptions explicit) the ways established interpretations and practices privilege certain groups (often at the expense of others). For example, in the New Testament women received the gospel and helped promote it. Women exercised a variety of roles in the New Testament church, including serving as missionaries, leaders, prophets, deacons, and apostles. As the church became part of the wider established culture, women's function and status in the early church were strongly influenced by the prevailing patriarchal form of family life. There, women's principal function was as wife and mother and as such they were subordinate to their fathers or husbands. Accepting the subordination of women to men, the New Testament writers stress the duty of modesty, submission, and piety. Domestic virtues become a woman's demonstration of piety and faith. Even as a postmodern approach leads Christians today to rejoice when voice and status are restored to those who have been discounted and dismissed, we may become resistant when we feel that our own contribution is devalued and we experience ourselves as displaced.

Fourth, postmoderns are eager to engage voices from the past to discover wisdom for negotiating the future. As I said, scholars see parallels between our time and that of the early church. The church today therefore looks to the earliest Christian communities for what they can teach us. For example, the renewal of worship in all mainline denominations since the Second Vatican Council of the Roman Catholic Church is based on the church's practices in the third and fourth centuries.[10]

By valuing experience, considering social location, challenging prevailing interpretations, and learning from the past, postmodernity invites faith communities and their leaders to listen to and talk with not only biblical texts and other communities but also the diverse voices and perspectives within their own faith communities as they seek insights into God's intention for our time. However, we may resist those voices when they challenge what we hold most dear, or we may attempt to control those voices to achieve our objectives.

Because people with a variety of perspectives are part of Christ's church, and even part of a single congregation, the members of

Christ's body cannot assume that their assumptions and convictions about the faith are universally held; rather, they need to be in conversation with one another for Christians and congregations to thrive and grow. Leadership is critical to such conversation. In her award-winning book *Leadership and the New Science: Discovering Order in a Chaotic World*, Margaret Wheatley argues that, inasmuch as "nothing happens until we observe it," organizations (including congregations) need lots of people looking—gathering data, views, and interpretations—because an "organization rich with many interpretations develops a wiser sense of what is going on and what needs to be done. Such organizations become more intelligent!"[11] Wheatley asserts that the leader's task is to create the conditions for people to develop a clear sense of what they are trying to accomplish and how they are trying to behave, so that people use this clear purpose to interpret information, experiences, and surprises. According to Wheatley, leaders "need to evoke contributions through freedom, trusting that people can make sense of information because they know their jobs, and they know the organizational or team purpose."[12] Similarly, Ronald A. Heifetz, cofounder of the Center for Public Leadership at the John F. Kennedy School of Government, Harvard University, asserts that one of the leader's principal responsibilities is to facilitate the learning required to address conflicts in the values people hold, or to diminish the gap between the values people stand for and the reality they face, to help them move ahead in addressing problems. Leaders ask whether making progress on a problem requires changes in people's values, attitudes, habits, or behavior.[13]

I have previously written that holy and active listening is essential if congregations and their pastors are to address and respond in a healthy and constructive manner to the questions and issues they face.[14] I describe holy and active listening as listening that invites others to share what they think, feel, and believe in order to discern together the presence and activity of God in their midst, because Christians expect God to speak in and through their conversation. Part of this listening involves Christians and congregations naming and owning the diverse assumptions that shape their shared faith and common life. Pastors and congregational leaders rightly observe that asking people to share their most cherished convictions, which may lead to conflict, is difficult when issues are controversial and stakes are high. They ask for a tool to help begin the dialogue in a way that is less intimidating. My own experience, together with that of the pastors and congregations with whom I have worked, suggests that, approached as an invitation to conversation, the Sunday sermon is the right tool.

The Sermon as Invitation to Conversation

The Sunday sermon is the principal means by which the church most closely relates the Christian faith to the daily lives of the vast majority of practicing Christians. Christians generally expect to be influenced by the sermons they hear. Some parishioners listen to sermons exclusively for direction for their individual lives. Other parishioners understand that sermons are addressed to everyone in the congregation and expect sermons to guide different people in different ways, though all in a similar direction. Still other listeners regard the sermon as the preacher speaking to the congregation in order to unite the faith community, to consider issues with the congregation, and to lead the congregation as a whole in a particular direction. For their part, some preachers appeal solely to individual lives, but most preachers address people both as individuals and as congregation members. A few preach to the congregation as a single community, God's covenant people.[15] Regardless of how preachers preach and parishioners listen, both preachers and people who listen to sermons expect preaching to influence their lives and congregations.

Preaching is also an effective way to deepen and enliven a congregation's mission and ministry. In its worship the faith community is most aware of its identity as God's people and its shared life in Christ. The greatest percentage of congregation members are present at worship, rather than at any meeting, class, discussion, or forum. More important, praying together, singing favorite hymns, and simply being in the worship space together centers people in the gospel and reinforces the congregation's sense of community. For these reasons, discussing people's experience and reactions to

sermons is a powerful way to discover the convictions they bring
to church.

Let's join an imaginary congregation, St. Ambrose Church, on
a particular Sunday. Pastor Mark longs to offer a decisive word
about what God is doing, while some congregants like Drew long
to receive an authoritative word about what they ought to think,
feel, and do. Christians like Fred, weary of the church's old answers, yearn for a new word. Others—people like Brian who have
been hurt, damaged, shamed, and rejected by the church's preaching but long for God—loiter on the church's front porch, afraid
to come inside. They pray that preaching will provide an experience of God that is loving and safe. Still others—people like Connie who revere Scripture and the sacred and resist pulling back
stained-glass curtains to examine their faith under the cold light
of day—desire preaching far removed from the concerns of the
world. Others, including Eleanor, accustomed to being deferred to
and obeyed, resent preaching that challenges the status quo and
silences their voices. Yet those long silenced, like Audrey, yearn
for preaching that encourages and empowers them to speak. Lisa,
full of faith and on fire for the gospel, cannot understand why the
church is slow to share the good news, while Gail encounters God
and grows in faith quite apart from preaching.

People like those just described are members of every Christian
congregation. Even in congregations of the same Christian tradition, members hold differing convictions because of their different
life circumstances, religious experiences, theological perspectives,
and beliefs. In the chapters that follow, these members of St. Ambrose Church share how their lives shape both their faith and their
understanding of preaching.

The members of St. Ambrose Church are based on my experience, both direct and indirect, in countless congregations. Given a
framework and tools for conversation, preachers and parishioners
will eagerly discuss sermons that describe how the Christian faith
can actually be lived by contemporary Christians and will lament
sermons that leave the impression that the Christian faith is disconnected from or unrelated to real life. When faith communities
discuss their reactions to sermons, as well as what they think and
how they feel about preaching, they eventually discover and re-

Figure I.I. The Sermon Discussion Group at St. Ambrose Church

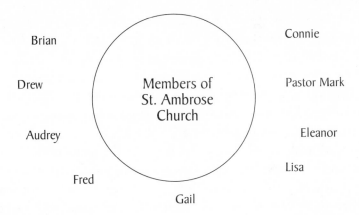

Brian

Connie

Drew

Members of
St. Ambrose
Church

Pastor Mark

Audrey

Eleanor

Lisa

Fred

Gail

flect upon the beliefs and convictions they bring to church. Talking about preaching invites and empowers members of congregations to identify and share the convictions about their faith that occupy their hearts.

More than shaping how the sermon is preached and heard, these convictions influence how Christians live in the world and the ways faith communities worship, function, and serve together. For example, in one congregation the pastor so taught that evangelism means "making disciples" that some people felt telling people what to do was the only way of legitimately sharing their faith. Uncomfortable with this, the congregation responded with apathy if not outright resistance. One Sunday a guest preacher delivered a sermon about evangelism as "proclaiming the nearness of the reign of God." Several congregants reported that, because they were uncomfortable "making disciples" by telling people what to do, a different understanding of what it means to share their faith—such as assuring people that God is near them—freed them to do so.

When sermons surface diverse voices in communities of faith on such topics as evangelism, social and ethical issues, and interpretations of Scripture or church doctrine, parish pastors and congregational leaders can either attempt to smooth those differences over or bring them out into the open. Pastors and congregations daring enough to air different perspectives revealed by

preaching find that, once people share their convictions and perspectives in a nonthreatening manner, congregations can move
beyond discussing preaching and consider together how their diverse voices inform the issues they face and shape the mission and
ministry they share.

The value of such conversation is evident in the preachers and
members of congregations who are attempting to recapture the
spirit of Acts through what teachers of preaching call a "conversational" approach to preaching. In this approach, preacher and
congregation discover God's message for them together. Preaching professor Lucy Atkinson Rose describes the goal of preaching as gathering the community of faith around the Word where
the central conversations of the church are refocused and fostered.
"In conversational preaching," Rose writes, "the preacher and the
congregation are colleagues, exploring together the mystery of the
Word for their own lives, as well as the life of the congregation,
the larger church, and the world."[16] The partners in Rose's model
of conversational preaching include God, the gathered community of believers, the church in its various configurations, biblical
texts and the witness of historic faith communities, people who are
marginalized or silenced, and the world. Some faith communities
undertake conversational preaching through discussions aimed at
providing input and feedback to sermons; others experiment to
discover ways to make the sermon an actual conversation. Regardless of their approach, these faith communities recognize the
potential of using people's experiences and expectations of preaching as a catalyst for identifying and discussing their Christian convictions and the ways these convictions shape their mission and
ministry. People are eager for tools that help them facilitate this
conversation. This book is one such tool.

The questions that bring this introduction to a close are intended to help members of your congregation discuss together
whether you consider the approach of this book valid and helpful. Specifically, do you agree that diverse faith convictions are an
inherent part of your congregation and the church? Do you agree
that preaching surfaces this diversity and that discussing preaching
can help your congregation respond to it in a life-giving manner?

Before answering the questions that follow, this might also be a good time for your group to agree on the "rules of engagement" that will govern your conversation. I established several rules that governed my own thinking as I wrote this book. First, in this conversation, people's convictions about their faith are neither wrong nor right. Second, I try to approach tension as an opportunity to discover how and where the Spirit is leading. A third rule is that people who discuss this book treat one another as co-learners. When you are ready, I invite you in chapter 1 to consider whether preaching is leadership.

Questions for Discussion

- In what ways, if any, do you consider yourself postmodern? Give examples of ways your congregation is and is not postmodern.
- How do you connect your faith and everyday life? Do you agree that most practicing Christians use the Sunday sermon to help them do so? Why or why not?
- Is there an issue or a topic that you find difficult to discuss in church? Can you name it to your conversation partners?
- Whom do you most identify with among the listeners described on pages 8 and 9?
- What do you think of the notion that tension in church is an opportunity to discern the Holy Spirit?
- How do your congregation and pastor discuss preaching and give and receive input and feedback on sermons?
- What rules of engagement will govern your conversation?

Chapter One

Is Preaching Leadership?

Is preaching leadership? At St. Ambrose Church, Audrey is contemplating a major life decision, a career change. Do you think Audrey can go to church expecting Pastor Mark to say something in the sermon that informs, guides, or directs her decision making? Do you think Pastor Mark expects the sermon he preaches to impact Audrey's life in a significant way? Does Pastor Mark have a particular hope or outcome in mind? Suppose St. Ambrose Church finds itself in financial difficulty, with expenses exceeding income. Should members of the congregation expect sermons that speak to the situation in a way that leads the congregation forward? Or should they look for this kind of leadership somewhere else?

In the introduction to this book, I outlined several reasons why the Sunday sermon is the chief way most practicing Christians connect their faith and daily lives. Because this is the case, the Sunday sermon is the most important opportunity and venue for the church, through its preachers, to lead both individuals and communities of faith. Preaching influences how pastors and other leaders attempt to guide both individuals and congregations in at least two ways. The Sunday worship service is where the vast majority of people have the most intentional and sustained contact with their pastor. By listening to sermons, many people determine whether their pastor is their spiritual and congregational leader. Based on what they experience in the sermon, many people not only decide whether the pastor is faithful, caring, and competent, but they also conclude whether their pastor has a vision, a direction for the congregation's ministry, and can inspire people to participate in it. People also use the Sunday sermon to assess what the congregation claims to believe and stand for, to determine whether the congregation's actions and leadership are consistent with its articulated values.

Yet the question of whether preaching is leadership is bigger than assessing how accurately preaching allows congregational members to size up their pastor as a leader. The question is bigger than whether pastors and other church leaders can and should take advantage of a "captive audience" by using the pulpit or sermon time for other leadership activities to achieve a particular outcome or to move the congregation in a certain direction. The question is bigger than whether the preaching of a particular pastor in a given congregation is leadership. *Is preaching the gospel in and of itself leadership?* Will "the news (revealed through Israel and confirmed for the church through Jesus Christ) of the promise of God's unconditional love for each and every created entity and the call of God for justice (that is relationships of love and abundance) for each and for all"[1] change, motivate, and empower people? Can the proclamation of the good news "that God's love, confirmed in Jesus Christ, is freely, graciously, offered to each and all, and . . . that we are to love God with our whole selves and to love and do justice to our neighbors as ourselves"[2] guide and direct people? Set aside all those times when preaching fails to live up to its potential and we can point to valid reasons why it does not motivate, direct, and guide. When preaching is flawless, when a sermon is everything it could possibly be, is preaching leadership? The answer is key to the conversation this book and your congregation are undertaking. If preaching is leadership, becoming aware of the convictions people bring to the sermon enhances preaching's leadership potential. If it is not, talking about preaching, while edifying, is irrelevant to individual and congregational lives. The answer to the question of whether preaching is leadership depends, in part, on whether we regard Jesus as our leader.

Is Jesus Our Leader?

Is Jesus our leader? We call Jesus our savior, lord, teacher, friend, shepherd, and even our king. But at work, at school, in our families, in our business dealings, at church council meetings, do we consider Jesus our leader? Or, do we follow someone or something else? To what extent does Jesus lead our worship, our politics, and our ethics? To what degree does Jesus lead our career, finances, and relationships? Put another way, how much do we believe the gospel we hear and preach? If, as Paul declares, "the message about the cross is . . . the power of God,"[3] how much do we trust and expect this power to work in our lives, in our congregations, and in the world? Do we believe the gospel can convert us, can change us again and again and again?

These questions are germane to whether preaching is leadership, because the church believes that it preaches following Jesus's example, in obedience to Jesus's command, and by Jesus's authority. If we do not regard Jesus as our leader, we will look for some other leader's example, direction, and authority, which will most likely involve an approach to leadership other than preaching. If we accept Jesus as our leader, we can consider how preaching is leadership by examining how definitions of leadership relate to Jesus's own preaching and the implications of that relationship for the preaching of the church. If we consider Jesus our leader, we can learn about the relationship of preaching and leadership from Jesus, who preached himself, commanded the church to preach, and is the power at work in preaching. To do this, you and I will spend time in this chapter reflecting on Jesus's preaching ministry and the ways it is leadership.

But what does *leadership* mean? Everyone, especially those who study leadership, has opinions about what constitutes leadership and what makes a good leader. Ronald A. Heifetz offers four prominent, common connotations of *leadership*. Heifetz reports that people understand leadership as the process of influence between a leader and followers to attain organizational objectives, the ability to provide the managerial functions associated with positions of senior authority, having a vision and getting people to realize it, and the ability to include others, particularly by noncoercive means.[4] Beginning with these common understandings and refining them using the insights of both experts in leadership and my own experience as pastor and congregational consultant, I use five definitions of leadership to examine Jesus's preaching. Leadership is (1) influencing others,

Figure 1.1. Definitions of Leadership

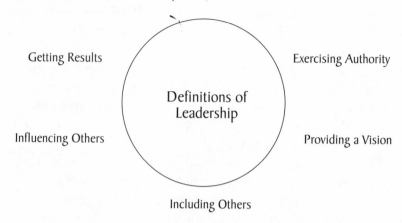

(2) exercising authority, (3) providing a vision, (4) getting results, and (5) including others.

Using verbs to describe these notions of leadership highlights
that leadership is an activity. Heifetz defines leadership as "the
activity of a citizen from any walk of life mobilizing people to do
something."[5] This definition helps clarify common understandings
of leadership. Here note the word *activity* in Heifetz's definition.
In this book, I am talking about preaching itself and not the status
of either the preacher or the congregation, though these certainly
influence preaching, particularly the preaching of Jesus.

Influencing Others

A prominent connotation of leadership is *influencing others*. Leadership is the process of influence between a leader and followers to
attain organizational objectives. Leaders draw people along and
precede them to an actual or a metaphorical destination. Leadership is influencing people to do or to believe something. At the
same time, the way people respond influences how leaders draw
them along.

That Jesus influenced people is clear from the Gospel reports
that Jesus's ministry garnered him followers. In addition to the
twelve apostles and the women who accompanied Jesus, great
crowds followed Jesus.[6] Disciples left their nets to follow him. The

crowds were so influenced by Jesus that, though the chief priests and scribes sought to kill Jesus, they were afraid to do so because of Jesus's followers.[7] The soldier who watched Jesus die was so moved that he proclaimed, "Truly this man was God's Son!"[8]

Jesus's ways of influencing people to live and believe the gospel include preaching, teaching, healing, performing miracles, reaching out to people on the margins, rubbing those in authority the wrong way, dying on a cross, and rising from the dead. The first thing to note about preaching the gospel as leadership is that Jesus's ministry of the word is part of the larger process Christ uses to influence people to have faith and love God and neighbor. Similarly, in most congregations, preaching alone cannot inspire and mobilize a congregation to greater ministries. Rather, preaching must both be partnered with forms of leadership that involve congregational leaders in addition to the pastor and be supported by the other aspects of congregational life. The annual stewardship sermon, for example, does not stand by itself but is one of many ways congregational leaders influence members to grow in their giving and to meet the congregation's mission goals.

Jesus certainly considered himself a preacher, and so does the church. When we examine the Gospel accounts of Jesus's ministry, first in Galilee and then in Jerusalem, we find that, more than anything else, Jesus was an itinerant preacher.[9] Mark's portrait of Jesus gives the impression that preaching was the primary emphasis of Jesus's ministry. Mark starts his account of Jesus's ministry by declaring, "Jesus came to Galilee, proclaiming the good news of God, and saying, 'The time is fulfilled, and the kingdom of God has come near; repent, and believe in the good news.'" Mark then describes what we might call a "preaching tour" in Galilee.[10] Jesus tells the disciples that they are leaving Nazareth to go on to the neighboring towns so that he might also proclaim the message there; for, according to Jesus, that is what he came to do. We might think of preaching as the seed of Jesus's earthly ministry from which everything else grows. Using Mark's language, Jesus's preaching is like a mustard seed, which, when sown, is the smallest of all the seeds; yet it grows and becomes the greatest of all.[11]

By following Jesus's example, we can see that preaching is central to the church's leadership. The church cannot divorce preaching from leadership, either by ministers approaching the preaching task as perfunctory while investing in other "more important" leadership activities or by congregations replacing the sermon with what they regard as a more effective form of leadership, such as a campaign for some congregational program or the presentation of a particular agenda. These attempts at leadership frequently do not succeed, because they are not informed and supported by the proclamation of the gospel. Congregational members listening for this gospel proclamation and not hearing it come to expect less of sermons and may even stop coming to church altogether. When this happens, preaching is still leading, but in such cases preaching is leading away.

Both Matthew and Luke make clear that neither Jesus's preaching nor the preaching of the church is an original word. Rather, Christian preaching is a continuation of God's ongoing speech. For Matthew, Jesus is the preacher who completely fulfills the priestly role of teaching the Law of Moses and the prophetic role of proclaiming the word of God. This balance of the Law and the Prophets is most evident in Matthew's account of the transfiguration, where the disciples see that Jesus was the one who spoke to Moses on Mount Sinai and from whom Elijah heard the still, small, prophetic voice on the same mountain.[12] In Luke, Jesus inaugurates his ministry by preaching that the Spirit of the Lord has anointed him to preach good news to the poor, recovery of sight to the blind, release to the captives, and liberty to the oppressed.[13] Jesus's preaching is a continuation of the prophetic words he has just read. All four Gospels make this point explicit by showing that Jesus's preaching followed from the preaching of John the Baptist, which followed in the tradition of the preaching of the prophets. As leadership, preaching is influential when it is a word given by God that is in keeping with God's recognized and recorded speech to humanity.

At the same time, Jesus's preaching is distinct. While the prophets preach hope and repentance, Jesus grounds hope and repentance in the good news that the promises of God have been fulfilled. The section "Providing a Vision" below describes how, in both Mark and Luke, Jesus announces that the appointed or acceptable time has come and the promises of God are being fulfilled. In this same way, the church proclaims a distinctive variation on God's theme of fulfillment in Christ. This variation is characterized by balance—law and prophets, freedom and accountability, God's gift of grace in Christ and the gospel's call to respond to that gift in faith. These variations are also appropriate to the faith community and to the occasion; in Luke, Jesus preached his inaugural sermon in the synagogue at Nazareth, his hometown. The sermon reflects the uniqueness of the situation. Jesus recognizes that the congregation has special expectations of him and of what he should say and do for them, and he even anticipates the congregation's response.[14]

The Gospel of John makes even more prominent the point that preaching is a variation on God's theme of fulfillment in Christ. It does so by presenting Jesus as the word of God become flesh, who from all eternity was with God and actually is God.[15] John's use of the word *logos* (word), which first of all means something said, makes plain how profoundly this Gospel writer regarded the reading and preaching of Scripture in worship. Jesus is the Word of God as it had been read and preached in Israel ever since the time of Moses and as it continues to be read and preached in the worship of the Christian church. As the law was given through Moses as the word of God, so grace and truth are given to us in Jesus Christ. Jesus, then, is "God's sermon preached to us in the living out of a human life."[16] In the preaching of Jesus, God begets children of God and gives them eternal life. The church's preaching is nothing other than witnessing to, unfolding, and interpreting this sermon.

Finally, Jesus's preaching shows us that, at times, preaching may not be influential at all. John reports that after Jesus finished preaching the Discourse on the Bread of Life, "many of his disciples turned back and no longer went about with him." Even more obvious, Luke reports that Jesus's preaching caused the people of Nazareth to drive him out of the town and lead him to the brow of the hill on which their town was built, "so that they might hurl him off the cliff."[17]

What we know to be true for the preaching of Jesus is even truer for the preaching of the church. Sometimes preaching does not influence people at all. While the good news of God's unconditional love and acceptance certainly attracts people, the

call to discipleship and the demands of the gospel cause many to
turn away. Jesus makes this point explicitly in his Sermon to the
Disciples.[18] Jesus directs that, when people do not listen, the
preacher is to move on to the next town. Put another way, the
church is to keep preaching. More important, preachers and congregations should not be surprised by rejection and even persecution. When persecuted, both the preacher and the congregation
are upheld by God's protecting hand, for God's eye is on God's
people in the same way that God watches the sparrow. Remembering this helps both preachers and parishioners pause to assess
whether we are measuring our ministry of the word in terms of
its popularity and worship attendance. At times, faithfulness to
the gospel demands that a congregation's ministry of the word
will be difficult to hear and preach and may cause some people
to turn away. Like Jesus, we may need to be ready and willing to
allow people to fall away, rather than compromise the gospel we
preach. Preaching always influences people, but not always in the
ways either preachers or listeners expect.

Exercising Authority

People look to leaders to *exercise the authority of their position
or office.* Heifetz reports that a second prominent connotation of
leadership is the ability to provide the managerial functions associated with positions of senior authority. While we regard preaching
as a function of Jesus's position as Messiah or Son of God, the Gospels also reveal that Jesus preached as one recognized as a teacher
or rabbi. Luke's account of the boy Jesus in the temple[19] indicates
that Jesus prepared for his ministry of preaching in the same way
that any Jewish boy in first-century Galilee would. While it may
have been unusual for a boy Jesus's age to ask questions and for all
who heard him to be amazed at his understanding, sitting among
the teachers and listening to them is how one prepared to become
a teacher. Jesus trained for an office. As part of his description of
Jesus's first sermon in Nazareth, Luke reports that Jesus went to
the synagogue on the Sabbath and was asked to preach. This was
not an impromptu invitation. Preachers normally were expected

to prepare and were therefore given the time necessary to do so. This customary practice indicates that people regarded Jesus as holding the office of preacher or teacher. Matthew's account of the Sermon on the Mount likewise indicates that Jesus had the honor and position of a recognized teacher. Jesus sat on a mountain while he preached; not only did Jesus physically assume the position of a rabbi but also his hearers would not have missed the allusion to Mount Sinai and Israel's greatest teacher. Similarly, the Sermon on Last Things begins with Jesus sitting and the disciples coming to him, the position of a recognized teacher.[20]

Jesus not only carried out a ministry of preaching himself, but he also made a point of establishing the office of preaching. Jesus called to himself disciples whom he trained to continue this ministry and sent out into all the world to preach the same gospel. Both before and after the resurrection, Jesus extended his own preaching ministry by empowering and authorizing the disciples, and after them the church, to preach in his name. Mark tells us that Jesus "went up the mountain and called to him those whom he wanted, and they came to him. And he appointed twelve, whom he also named apostles, to be with him, and to be sent out to proclaim the message, and to have authority to cast out demons." In Luke, Jesus not only sends the twelve apostles; Jesus appoints seventy others, and sends them ahead in pairs to every place he intends to go.[21] When Jesus appointed messengers, whether twelve or seventy, and sent them to proclaim the gospel, he initiated the Office of the Ministry of the Word. That the apostolic church understood Christ appointed the apostles to this office is evident in Acts 10:32-43. According to Luke, Peter preached that Jesus commanded the apostles to testify to his ministry, death, and resurrection and to preach that God appointed Jesus to judge the living and the dead.

Jesus trained those whom he appointed and sent to preach. The Gospels offer glimpses of this training, including Jesus's assessment of their mission and his "marching orders" as he sends them.[22] For Luke, announcing that the Scriptures of the Old Testament have been fulfilled is essential to preaching the gospel. Jesus trains the disciples to preach that Christ's victory over death was according to Scripture. The disciples are sent to explain Scripture as Jesus himself explained Scripture to them.[23]

Jesus also invested this office with tremendous authority. Jesus gave those he had appointed and sent power and authority over all demons and to cure diseases. Jesus charged them to proclaim the good news that the reign of heaven has come near, to cure the sick, to raise the dead, to cleanse the lepers, and to cast out demons.[24] Casting out demons and other mighty works are God-given signs that confirm the apostles' preaching of the gospel, just as some Christian traditions understand the healing, forgiveness, faith, and new life that Christians receive in Baptism and the Lord's Supper as confirming the church's preaching of the gospel. They indicate that the reign of God has come near. Most significant, Jesus promises that, in the proclamation of Christian preachers, people come into direct fellowship with Christ. Jesus tells the seventy, "Whoever listens to you listens to me, and whoever rejects you rejects me, and whoever rejects me rejects the one who sent me."[25]

Turning from the apostles to the church, Matthew reports that, after the resurrection, Jesus commissions the eleven, and with them the church, to teach—"baptizing them in the name of the Father and of the Son and of the Holy Spirit, and teaching them to obey everything that I have commanded you." Yet, Mark uses a different word to describe the fulfillment of this command: "And they went out and proclaimed the good news everywhere, while the Lord worked with them and confirmed the message by the signs that accompanied it."[26] Preaching and teaching are synonymous in the New Testament. The disciples sent out by Jesus "to proclaim the message" returned and told Jesus "all that they had done and taught."[27]

Paul also treats preaching and teaching as the same. When Paul says that God decided to save those who believe through the foolishness of the church's proclamation,[28] it is not clear whether Paul was speaking about the absurdity of the act of preaching or of the absurdity of the message preached. Throughout the New Testament, while proclamation itself is the primary dynamic activity of preaching, the content of the message is always included within the general connotation of the term. Preaching or proclamation, then, is both act and message. In this sense, Christ can promise to be present in the teaching of disciples "until the end of the age," and Mark can observe that "the Lord worked with them and confirmed the message."[29] The efficacious and mysterious presence of Christ is the final Word and power at work in the preaching and teaching of both Christ's disciples and the church. Without the presence of Jesus, preaching lacks both inspiration and authority.

Essential to preaching as exercising authority is remembering that the authority of the office of preaching rests on God's creative, enlightening word and is not the possession of the preacher. Jesus makes plain that preaching is divine work, and preachers are instruments in God's employ. Jesus reminds preachers that it is not they who speak but the Spirit of God speaking through them. Preaching—both the word the preacher receives and the message the congregation hears—is gratuitous in that it is grace-filled, freely given by God.[30] While both preacher and congregation prepare for the proclamation of the gospel, the message is not contrived or programmed. Rather the preacher is overcome by God's grace and offers a fearless profession of faith based on a wholehearted commitment to Christ.[31] Thus the authority to preach rests on God's call and God's word. Because God's reign is governed by God's word, Christ's representatives are responsible for serving God by hearing, reading, interpreting, and witnessing to God's Word rather than to speak for or rely upon themselves. The congregation is called as much as the preacher is called. Preaching only happens when a congregation regards a preacher as an authentic representative of Christ. Regardless of their clerical status, preachers have no authority to preach in a congregation that will not listen to them. Thus the authority of God's word comes to the preacher through the congregation.

Today preaching remains one of a few responsibilities expressly accorded to the pastoral office, and even this is changing. Historically, pastors are explicitly called to preach, lead worship, provide pastoral care and visitation, teach the faith, and respond to those in need. Today many clergy seek and many congregations expect their pastor to carry out leadership responsibilities for which clergy may be neither qualified nor authorized, including functioning as congregational CEO, facility manager, community organizer, fund-raiser, or financial analyst. Preaching nonetheless remains the predominant expectation of clergy. When a pastor unsuccessfully carries out responsibilities associated with other

roles or does so in way the congregation does not expect or support, the pastor's leadership changes and may be diminished as
other leaders reclaim these responsibilities, but in spite of the
lack of success, the pastoral relationship continues. Alternatively,
however, when a pastor is unsuccessful as a preacher or loses the
authority to preach God's word in a congregation, the pastoral
relationship is effectively terminated. To preserve and enhance
the fundamental responsibility of the pastoral office, other areas
of congregational leadership might best be carried out by qualified members of the congregation as an expression of the priest-
hood of all believers, freeing the pastor to lead by preaching the
gospel.

Providing a Vision

Particularly in congregations desiring to grow, people understand
leadership is *having a vision and getting people to realize it.* According to this definition, leadership involves (1) having a vision
and (2) getting results. The first task is considered here and the
second in the next section. A vision for mission is a clear mental
picture of a preferable future, imparted by God to God's people,
that grows from an accurate understanding of God, self, and circumstances.[32] Those who study leadership describe the way an organization achieves its goals in terms of organizational purpose
and vision rather than positional power.

Jesus illustrates that leadership comes from vision rather than
position when he says: "You know that the rulers of the Gentiles
lord it over them, and their great ones are tyrants over them. It will
not be so among you; but whoever wishes to be great among you
must be your servant, and whoever wishes to be first among you
must be your slave; just as the Son of Man came not to be served
but to serve, and to give his life a ransom for many."[33] With this
powerful vision, Jesus replaces the power that comes from holding
a position.

The vision of Jesus's preaching ministry can be described as
fulfillment. Jesus came onto the scene "proclaiming the good news
of God, and saying, 'The time is fulfilled, and the kingdom of God
has come near; repent, and believe in the good news.'"[34] The first

priority of Jesus's preaching ministry is announcing the good news that the promises of Scripture are fulfilled and the long-promised reign of God is at hand. Jesus recounts the promises of God and their fulfillment in himself by teaching the Scriptures and announcing in word and deed the good news that they are being fulfilled in him. Only in light of this revelation does Jesus call people to faith and faithfulness. The vision of fulfillment is also prominent in Luke's account of Jesus's sermon at Nazareth, which begins Jesus's preaching ministry in that Gospel. Jesus's sermon is basically the announcement that the prophecy he just read is fulfilled. Jesus declares, "Today this scripture has been fulfilled in your hearing."[35] Fulfillment can also be understood as the overarching vision of the Sermon on the Mount. This vision of fulfillment is set by the Beatitudes, which for Matthew is the keynote of all Jesus's preaching. Jesus gives good news to the poor in spirit, those who mourn, the meek, those who hunger and thirst for righteousness, the pure in heart, peacemakers, and those who are persecuted.[36] Then Jesus teaches the crowds how to live in God's reign.

For preaching to provide leadership, congregations and their preachers need a vision for their ministry of the word that flows from and is congruent with Jesus's own vision of proclaiming the gospel, *fulfillment*. This vision informs and guides both sermons and all the other ways congregations proclaim the gospel. Some visions come from Scripture; John 3:16 is an example. Other visions are reflected in a congregation's denominational affiliation; Lutherans use justification by grace through faith. Other visions of proclaiming the gospel grow out of a congregation's experience of God; its situation or circumstances; or its theological questions, convictions, and concerns. In chapter 7, you and I will consider visions of proclaiming the gospel as we discuss the church's mission. Here in chapter 1 our focus is the importance of a vision of proclaiming the gospel for both the Sunday sermon and a congregation's ministry of the word.

Getting Results

Of course, having a vision is leadership only when the leader can get people to realize that vision. Some people measure leadership using the yardstick of results; a leader is the person who is most successful. Heifetz's own definition indicates that leadership is "the activity of . . . mobilizing people to do something." For Heifetz, the "something" that leaders mobilize people to do is "adaptive work," which consists of "the learning required to address conflicts in the values people hold, or to diminish the gap between the values people stand for and the reality they face," in order to help them move ahead in addressing problems. Leaders ask whether making progress on a problem requires changes in people's values, attitudes, habits, or behavior.[37]

This is a wonderful way to describe the effect of Jesus's preaching and, indeed, of Jesus's entire ministry. Jesus mobilized people to change their values, attitudes, habits, and behavior because, through Jesus's preaching, they understood and experienced God differently. Imagine the life-changing impact of coming to believe that God, rather than one who doles out favor according to how well people obey the law of Moses, is like someone who, having a hundred sheep and losing one of them, leaves the ninety-nine in the wilderness and goes after the one that is lost until he finds it. God is like a woman who has ten silver coins and loses one; she lights a lamp, sweeps the house, and searches carefully until she finds it. God is like a father who, seeing a returning son, even a son who wished him dead and wasted his inheritance, is filled with compassion, runs to his son, embraces and kisses him, and puts a robe on his back and a ring on his finger. When they find what was lost, all three throw a big party.[38] Luke indicates that people's new understanding and experience of God mobilized them to approach the world and their problems differently. Ten lepers and a man who was blind cried out for mercy, and Zacchaeus climbed down from his tree.[39]

People certainly expected Jesus's preaching to accomplish concrete results, most notably the overthrow of the Roman Empire and the restoration of the nation of Israel. But John reports that, after feeding the multitudes, Jesus withdrew by himself when he realized that the crowds were about to come and take him by force to make him king, and Jesus tells Pilate, "My kingdom is not from this world."[40] Even Jesus's closest followers expected results other than what Jesus accomplished. Both Matthew and Mark report that Peter rebuked Jesus when Jesus predicted the results of his ministry would be rejection, suffering, death, and resurrection.[41] In this same way, many clergy and laity berate preaching for not generating results, even as they preach and listen to sermons. Their concern is that the church seems to feed itself with God's word but never do anything. Frustrated parishioners complain about the poor preaching at the same time frustrated pastors complain that people are stuck in their ways and refuse to listen.

Heifetz helps us understand this defeat both among Jesus's first followers and in our own congregations, by distinguishing between "technical" and "adaptive" work.[42] When a problem is clear and both the solution and means of implementing it are obvious, organizations and their leaders undertake the "technical work" of carrying out the solution. Preaching is a less effective means of leadership in these situations. However, when defining the problem and identifying and implementing a solution depend upon an organization learning new values, attitudes, and habits of behavior, preaching is an effective way to lead congregations in this "adaptive work." Preaching articulates how the gospel informs and shapes attitudes and actions in the situation in which Christians find themselves. Preaching seeks to help people frame the problem using the gospel and identify all possible faithful responses so that the congregation can discern together which is best. In keeping with Heifetz's definition of a good leader, a good preacher asks whether the values of the gospel and the realities of the situation require changes in people's values, attitudes, and behavior. Like the first followers of Jesus, contemporary Christians become frustrated when the problem is clear to them, the solution is obvious, and preaching intentionally does not undertake the technical work that will produce those results. Yet, if the problem and solution are apparent to everyone, preaching does not need to address them.

When we approach the Sermon on the Parables as Jesus preaching about the ministry of the word, we glean important insights into the results we can expect preaching the gospel to generate. The parable of the sower is about the fruitfulness of proclaiming the gospel: by the grace of God, the preaching of the gospel will have tremendous success, despite the hardness of human hearts, persecution, and the cares of the world. The parable of the wheat and the tares assures us that preaching the gospel will bear fruit even when competing gospels are proclaimed. Like the sowing of the grain of mustard seed, which produced the tallest of trees, the preaching of the gospel will produce significant, though surprising, results. Perhaps most important, preaching is like yeast; it has a power, which may appear insignificant but has tremendous effect.

In this sermon, Jesus preaches the parables of the sower and the wheat and the tares to the crowds and then privately explains them to the disciples. Christian truth is not always grasped in first hearing; it needs to be listened to carefully and repeatedly. Congregations and preachers need to remember that mobilizing people to adapt new values, attitudes, and behavior takes time. Adaptive work is slow in coming; a single sermon will rarely do the job. I find no indication in the Gospels that any one of Jesus's sermons permanently changed people's lives. Even Peter's sermon at Pentecost, which generated three thousand converts,[43] must be understood as a continuation of Jesus's preaching and not an isolated proclamation.

When it comes to results, we do better to think of the cumulative effect of preaching, the small but significant ways sermons change people and faith communities over weeks, years, and lifetimes. Just as one snapshot has only a minimal influence on the observer's view of the subject but a collection of artistic photographs can change one's perspective, so the single sermon rarely overturns the hearer's worldview. The cumulative effect of small, transforming conversions, however, makes preaching an immensely important part of the church's ministry.[44]

Jesus demonstrated that he understood the cumulative effect of preaching when he appointed seventy preachers and sent them ahead in pairs to every place he intended to go.[45] Jesus emphasized that the proclamation of the word is part of a greater ministry and not an individual undertaking. No one fulfills the whole of this ministry alone; rather, preachers enter into the ministry of other laborers. Thus, the ministry of the word requires a company of ministers who work together, whether the pairs of preachers that Jesus sent out or the company of ministers preaching in a congregation's pulpit and people's lives over the course of many years.

The preaching that takes place in the pulpit must also be partnered with the preaching of all Christians who speak the gospel with words, through relationships, and in how the congregation lives.

While preachers in pulpits and parishioners who speak the gospel in their daily lives all have their own talents, God, "the Lord of the harvest,"[46] brings in the harvest. Paul makes this same point when he writes, "I planted, Apollos watered, but God gave the growth."[47] This recognition helps all ministers of the word faithfully proclaim the gospel and not panic when the time is not ripe and they do not see results, because, ultimately, the outcome is in God's hands.

Including Others

A fifth prominent connotation of leadership is the ability to *include others*, particularly by noncoercive means. Though many Christians understand proclaiming the gospel as something the professional clergy do for members of the congregation, those who study leadership demonstrate the necessity of including others, so that all people exercise leadership in an organization such as a congregation. Heifetz distinguishes between leadership and authority, which he defines as "conferred power to perform a service." Heifetz argues that unhinging leadership from position and personality trait allows us to observe "the many different ways in which people exercise leadership everyday without 'being leaders.'"[48] While those in authority are supposed to provide direction, protection, and order,[49] they frequently fail to do so. Then, people without authority are often the most effective leaders. Those without authority can deviate from the norms; raise questions that disturb; focus on a single issue; and be more attuned to people's hopes, pains, values, habits, and history.

In addition to offering a precise description of the way many congregational leaders function, Heifetz's observations about the ways those without authority lead provide a fine summary of Jesus's ministry. Jesus's own preaching illustrates the difference between leadership and authority. While preaching may be the function of an office, Jesus shows that proclaiming the gospel is not confined

to a particular position. We have seen that Jesus's preaching suc-
ceeded the preaching of John the Baptist and therefore fit into the
prophetic tradition of Israel. John the Baptist did not preach because society had given him that responsibility or because he held
an office. John was a charismatic preacher whom God's Spirit had
raised up, as God's Spirit had raised up the prophets, to preach
a unique message for a particular time. Jesus's preaching in the
temple is in keeping with this tradition. The prophets frequently
performed some symbolic act as an introduction to their preaching; Jesus's cleansing of and subsequent preaching in the temple is
the same sort of preaching. Matthew and Mark make the distinction between this kind of leadership and the authority of a position
or office by the way they describe the crowd's reaction to Jesus's
preaching. They report that, when Jesus finished preaching, the
crowds were astounded at his teaching, for he taught them as one
having authority, "and not as their scribes."[50]

Internationally recognized leadership consultant Margaret
Wheatley explains that "leadership is best thought of as a behavior, not a role" because roles are temporary; roles only last as long
as they facilitate the energy, relationships, and interactions that
make desired outcomes happen.[51] When that ceases to happen,
either the role itself or the person who holds the position changes.
Then someone else emerges from the group, not because of status
or self-assertion but because that person makes sense to the group
as one who can facilitate what is needed for the group and individuals within the group to survive and grow. Congregations might
seek a different type of preacher or preachers a different kind of
pulpit, but the activity of preaching continues. More significant,
in many circumstances the person best able to preach the gospel is
not the preacher with authority but the Christian friend, mentor,
coworker, congregational elder, or loved one.

That Jesus will not confine the work of the gospel to a particular role or office is evident in the account of another exorcist.
John reports to Jesus that the disciples saw someone casting out
demons in his name, and they tried to stop him because "he does
not follow with us." The unnamed exorcist was not one of the
group appointed to exercise authority in Jesus's name. But Jesus
tells John not to stop him, because no one who does a deed of

power in Jesus's name will be able soon afterward to speak evil of him. As Jesus sees it, "whoever is not against us is for us."[52] In this spirit, Wheatley writes, "We need all of us out there, stating, clarifying, reflecting, modeling, filling all of space with the messages we care about."[53] Heifetz calls leadership "the activity of a citizen from any walk of life."[54] Everyone exercises leadership, not just a special group.

That this is Jesus's intention is evident in the way Jesus preached throughout Galilee, Judea, and the country across the Jordan. Jesus not only preached in synagogues on the Sabbath, the equivalent of the Sunday sermon. Jesus also preached wherever he could gather a crowd. Jesus preached in the marketplace, on the mountainside, and beside the sea. Jesus reminds us that, while this book and the conversation it represents are concerned with the Sunday sermon, the church's ministry of the word, like that of Jesus, is more encompassing. Jesus preaching in the marketplace, beside the sea, and as he shared meals with people reminds us that Christians proclaim the gospel at home, at work, in school, on the street, and at play. Even in church, proclaiming the gospel is not limited to the sermon but includes hearing and studying Scripture, praying, singing hymns, fellowship, and service. Understood this way, preaching is not only the responsibility of pastors but of all the people of God.

The Gospel of John makes preaching by all Christians even more prominent.[55] Because God's ultimate revelation is a word, we can serve God in no higher way than to be ministers of that word. For John, the incarnation of the word leads to the proclamation of the word. In Jesus's High Priestly Prayer, we read, "For the words that you gave to me I have given to them."[56] Down through the centuries, the church's preaching of the gospel is nothing other than the word of God. Thus, Jesus prays, "I ask not only on behalf of these, but also on behalf of those who will believe in me through their word, that they may all be one."[57] Whatever our particular calling and vocation, John understands all Christians as ministers of God's word, though the form and location of our preaching differ. Our words respond to God's word in Christ. When our preaching reflects God's word in Jesus Christ, it possesses the tremendous authority of Christ our leader, the authority of the Word of God.

So how does the Sunday sermon include others in the church's larger ministry of proclaiming the gospel? Heifetz uses the word *mobilize* in his own definition of leadership: "the activity of a citizen from any walk of life mobilizing others to do something." To mobilize is to prepare and organize for service. Those who study leadership describe this preparation and organization using language, attitudes, and practices that transform and thereby mobilize. Leaders model the way and are prime encouragers of followers. Leaders empower others rather than force and pressure them. Wheatley emphasizes that leaders evoke contributions through freedom.[58]

Throughout the Gospels, Jesus chooses preaching to lead people to live and believe the gospel. Because we are so accustomed to thinking of Jesus as a preacher, we sometimes forget that Jesus could have used other perhaps more coercive means to lead his followers and carry out his mission. In Matthew's account of Jesus being tempted by the devil in the wilderness, Jesus specifically rejects three approaches to leadership that we might describe as manipulative and even coercive. Jesus could have pandered to people's needs and desires by preserving himself: "command these stones to become loaves of bread." Jesus could have forced God to act, and scared people into submission, through displays of power that shock and awe: "throw yourself down" from the pinnacle of the temple, and call down the angels who will bear you up on their hands, so that you will not dash your foot against a stone. Jesus could have allied himself with existing power structures to manipulate the system: "All [the kingdoms of the world and their splendor] I will give you, if you will fall down and worship me."[59] But Jesus chose preaching.

Charles Campbell, Professor of Homiletics at Columbia Theological Seminary in Decatur, Georgia, asserts that Jesus embodies God's way most specifically in his choice of preaching as his way of announcing the reign of God.[60] Both the form and the content of Jesus's preaching not only reveal Jesus's approach to leadership but they also declare who God is and how God works. By using preaching to announce God's reign, Jesus declares that God's way is neither silent passivity and acceptance nor coerced belief, forced agenda, and dominating control. Instead, Jesus's life and preaching allow humans the freedom of decision, choice, and expression. By using preaching to proclaim God's reign, Jesus requires and demonstrates mutuality. Receiving the kingdom involves both the one speaking and the ones listening. Jesus's preaching refuses to treat the listener as an object or commodity. Jesus's preaching does not coerce or control its outcome. Though other approaches certainly would have guaranteed greater success, Jesus chose to work through preaching, rather than through overwhelming temptation or absolute constraints, to inaugurate God's reign.

Like the preaching of Jesus, the church's preaching of the gospel does not attempt to control people or to force an outcome. Rather, the church teaches and trusts that God is at work in preaching. When, in faithfulness to the Scripture read in worship, the preacher proclaims our need of God's grace and freely offers that grace, the Spirit touches individual lives with God's grace and power and gathers and forms communities of faith to witness to Christ's love for the world. The word of God that is preached elicits from those who hear it a response. When the gospel is preached, that response is faith—trust in God's love in Christ. The leadership question is how preaching can and ought to make that faithful response concrete and specific. In whatever ways they choose, preachers endeavor to ensure that any explicit call for faithful response does not overshadow, undermine, or obscure the gospel in a way that people feel coerced by the erroneous notion that God's love depends upon their actions. Instead, preaching speaks to people's best selves, appealing to them as God's children, those claimed by Christ, filled with the Holy Spirit, and empowered for service by God's grace.

In this chapter, I offered five definitions of leadership and demonstrated how Jesus's preaching fulfills and illustrates them. I am convinced that the preaching of Jesus, as well as the church's proclamation of the gospel, is in and of itself leadership. Conversations that improve a congregation's ministry of the word enhance the sermon's potential as an expression of leadership. Yet, the sermon never stands alone. It is part of a congregation's overall ministry, particularly its worship, which is the subject of the next chapter.

Questions for Discussion

- Do you consider yourself a leader? Why or why not?
- What parts of your congregation's life and ministry does Jesus lead? Who or what leads the other parts?
- How do you know a good leader? What traits do you look for and appreciate?
- Do you agree that leadership is an activity or behavior of all people, rather than the role or position of some? Why or why not?
- How have you experienced the presence and power of Christ in preaching? Name a time when a sermon influenced you to do or believe something. Name a time that you turned away from or stopped listening to a sermon.
- How central is preaching to your congregation's and your pastor's ministry? How much time each week ought a preacher spend in sermon preparation?
- Describe your congregation's vision for its ministry of the word. How do you know a sermon has accomplished something? What sorts of results can we expect from preaching?
- What is the listener's responsibility in making the Sunday sermon leadership? If Connie desires preaching that is unrelated to life, can she expect preaching to be leadership?
- Do you agree that all Christians are called to be preachers? Why or why not? If you agree, where is your pulpit? To whom do you preach your best sermons?

Chapter Two

How Does the Sermon Fit in the Service?

Worship is arguably a congregation's primary purpose and activity, from which everything else the congregation is and does flows. Worship is what makes the church the church. In worship the Spirit gathers us as God's own. We hear God's word, receive God's love and forgiveness in Christ, and sing God's praise. Then the Spirit sends us to live as Christ's body in the world. In worship God draws us into God's own work of reconciliation, inspiring and empowering us to live and serve as Christ's body in the world. But what do we mean by *worship*?

Imagine going to a church some Sunday. Instead of music, prayers, Scripture reading, and singing, the minister enters the worship space, goes directly to the pulpit, and begins preaching. When the sermon is finished, the service is over; nothing more occurs. Would you say you had been to church? What more than a sermon do you need for what happens in church to be worship?

Though worship is essential to the church, churchgoers often talk about and even treat the sermon as a stand-alone event. Some congregations, preachers, and faith traditions begin the sermon with its own invocation and conclude the sermon with its own benediction. Yet, from Jesus's first sermon at Nazareth,[1] Christian preaching, like the preaching of the synagogue before it, has always been an accepted, a traditional, and a prescribed part of the worship service, even though the sermon is not included in some worship services. In fact, scholars argue that the inclusion of a sermon in the worship service, whether an oral lecture, personal testimony, or freely spoken word, is a trait that unites Judaism and Christianity. That a worship service is essential to preaching is evident in seminary preaching classes, which most certainly are not worship services. Students regularly reflect that their sermons are not "real" because they do not take place in the chapel as part of a worship service. Some students, when they preach in class, add an element of the worship service, such as a hymn or a prayer, to create the appropriate atmosphere and put their preaching in its proper context, making their sermons more "real."

So how does the sermon fit into the worship service? Today, the church teaches that the sermon is an integral part of the worship service. The Second Vatican Council of the Roman Catholic church asserted that "the homily . . . is to be highly esteemed as part of the liturgy itself; in fact, at those Masses which are celebrated with the assistance of the people on Sundays and feasts of obligation, it should not be omitted except for a serious reason." The current *United Methodist Book of Worship* calls for the Sunday service to be a "Service of Word and Table." The Evangelical Lutheran church in America's statement *The Use of the Means of Grace* asserts that "the two principal parts of the liturgy of Holy Communion, the proclamation of the Word of God and the celebration of the sacramental meal, are so intimately connected as to form one act of worship."[2]

Exodus 24:1-11 is a biblical example of the integration of sermon and worship service. Israel comes before God, and Moses reads and preaches the Scriptures of the covenant; then the elders go up on the mountain. They eat and drink and behold God. Just so, when the Christian assembly hears the reading and preaching of the Word and shares in the Lord's Supper, the gospel is sealed. The covenant assembly is united in communion with Christ.

In the New Testament, Jesus's Discourse on the Bread of Life teaches that we have covenant fellowship with the incarnate Word through both the preached word and the Lord's Supper. In both together Christ is truly present. We might say that this chapter speaks both of Christ's eucharistic presence and of Christ's kerygmatic presence, but we might better speak of the two together.[3] Through hearing the Word and participating in the sacraments, we enter into a covenantal union with Christ. Our fellowship with the Word of God gives us eternal life (John 6:57).

Luke's account of the road to Emmaus[4] provides a model of the integration of preaching and worship. Like the disciples traveling to Emmaus, we gather with Jesus, hear the Word spoken, receive the bread broken, and are sent with good news. In this way, Christ's presence in worship nourishes our faith and calls us to witness to the gospel. Generations of Christians have used this simple order of worship—gathering in song and prayer, confessing their need of God, reading the Scriptures and hearing them preached, praying and gathering an offering for the church's mission, remembering and celebrating Christ with bread and wine, receiving God's blessing, and being sent out in mission to the world.

Today the church and its teachers, including me, argue that the worship service is more than "a collection of liturgical knickknacks (e.g., hymns, prayers, passing the peace, the Lord's Supper) to set up the sermon, but should embody a coherent theological vision in its movement and practices, of which the sermon is a piece."[5] In response, many pastors and parishioners respond, "Yes, the most important piece." For some Christians and in some congregations, the sermon is the main event, for which everything else that happens in worship is decoration, a hint or an echo of the sermon. Luke describes Jesus's first sermon this way: Jesus goes to the synagogue, reads Scripture, preaches, and the service is immediately over as all speak well of him. Other Christians and congregations regard the sermon as an intermission from, if not an interruption of, the glorious music and ceremony that are the true heart of worship. For example, the sermon does not figure prominently in the heavenly worship described in Revelation 4:1-11, just as the sermon does not figure prominently in some festival, prayer, and choral services here on earth.

In most congregations, the way a sermon fits into a worship service changes a bit from Sunday to Sunday, even service to service. Many preachers understand that, on the most important festivals of the church year, such as Easter, people often do not come to church as much for the sermon as they do for the lilies and the music. People's main reason for attending weddings is certainly not to hear the sermon. Yet, on certain Sundays and other occasions, such as when the congregation faces a decision or individuals and the community experience a crisis like the unexpected or violent death of a loved one, people come to worship expressly for the sermon, to hear a word from the Lord.

Regardless of how worship and preaching fit together on any given Sunday, the worship service in most congregations includes preaching, and the sermon must fit with other elements of the service. More than passively providing the setting or circumstances in which preaching occurs, the worship service prepares the faith community for preaching; influences how the sermon is crafted, preached, and heard; and offers the first opportunity for the congregation to respond to the sermon.[6] Coming together as God's people, praising God, and reading and hearing Scripture together—generally the first parts of worship services that include preaching—prepares the preacher to preach, as well as the congregation to listen. Ideally, the congregation gathers around God's Word as a family gathers around its cherished stories. The Spirit uses the biblical account of God's salvation, proclaimed in worship, to unite the congregation in common identity as God's people and common purpose of praising God and serving the world. The sermon then relates this identity and purpose to life in the world.

The sermon is based on the Scripture that is read in a given worship service celebrated by a particular congregation. In addition to influencing how the preacher prepares the sermon, the worship service frequently provides a context through which the congregation hears the Scripture that is read. The worship context is perhaps more influential than a passage's context in the Bible. For example, more Christians associate the account of Jesus's birth in Luke 2 with carols, a tree, and candlelight—characteristics of the worship service when this passage is read—than with Zechariah's prophecy and Jesus being named, the stories that come before and after Jesus's birth in Luke's Gospel.

The worship service also directly influences the sermon itself in at least two ways. First, in some traditions, festivals like Good Friday and Easter and seasons such as Lent help preachers proclaim and congregations hear the gospel from different perspectives and with different emphases. Second, the style of the worship service certainly influences the style of the sermon. A sermon preached as part of a worship service designed for youth differs from the same message preached as part of a worship service at a senior living center. Even in the same congregation, word choices and delivery of essentially the same message differ at the liturgical and seeker services.

Finally, the congregation's first chance to respond to the sermon occurs in worship. Elements of the service, such as hymns, prayer, praise, offering, sacraments in some traditions and altar calls in others, reinforce the message of the sermon and provide the congregation with the words, actions, and opportunity to respond to that message in faith. Christians do not skip over these acts of worship or postpone responding to the sermon until they pass through the church door on their way out into the world. The sermon can either enhance or diminish the congregation's song, prayer, offering, and celebration in worship, however, which surely influences the congregation's service in the world.

Characteristics of Christian Worship

Before congregations can decide how sermons fit into their worship services, and how preaching and worship influence one another, congregations must determine what they mean by *worship*. As is the case with preaching, Christians and congregations bring a host of assumptions about what constitutes Christian worship with them to the service. At St. Ambrose Church, for example, Brian understands worship as an ordered progression of fixed components, while, for Connie, worship is a spontaneous spiritual experience. Drew values excellence over involvement, while Eleanor works hard to find ways to include everyone in leading the service or to recruit leaders who represent the entire congregation. For Fred, God through the church does something in worship; for Audrey, worship is something that people do for God. Rather than allowing these assumptions to catch us in conversation about "good" and "bad" or "right" and "wrong" worship, we can testify to the belief that "at all times and at all places the Holy Spirit helps us to pray (Rom. 8:26)."[7]

Liturgical historian James F. White's seven "categories" for analyzing Christian worship—people, piety, time, place, prayer, preaching, and music[8]—can help congregations talk about worship

Figure 2.1. Characteristics of Christian Worship

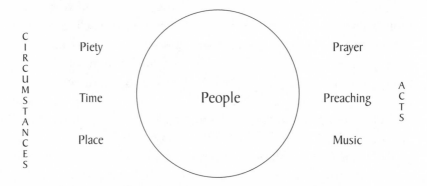

without getting caught in conversation about individual preferences. While these seven elements of a worship service certainly do not exhaust all possibilities, they provide a manageable set of reference points with which to organize conversation about worship. In addition to what is said, done, and sung in worship, White's categories invite people to consider the nature of the congregation's participation; the social life and personality of the participants; the ways sacred space is organized; visual and sound accompaniments; and the rhythm of the congregation's daily, weekly, yearly, and lifelong cycles. Some elements are more prominent in certain congregations and faith traditions than others and in some chapters of this book than others. Yet all are important and merit brief descriptions.

People

Frequently, the best way to understand worship is in terms of *people*. How do people's personalities and social lives affect worship? For example, whether people engage the world intellectually rather than emotionally and claim a large rather than a small personal space certainly impact both the form and the content of their worship and what they expect of a sermon. The chances are good that people who engage the world intellectually want preaching that is logical, rational, and academic.

Which characteristics of people must be taken into account in worship? For instance, the age of the people in a congregation might influence the kinds and amount of movement in worship. As one congregation aged, its Palm Sunday procession changed over the years from a congregational parade to a march of the Sunday school children to a symbolic procession of the ministers. People's age certainly influences what they listen for in sermons. Research indicates that, while the Greatest Generation listens for sermons that build up the church and help them live a better life, Baby Boomers want sermons to help them understand life as a whole, the Silent Generation wants sermons that build bridges among people, and Generation X desires sermons that relate the gospel to their experience.[9]

Next, in what way do people participate in worship? Are they passive or receptive, as people watch or listen to someone else do something, or active, as people pray, sing, shout, and move themselves? A congregation that participates in preaching by listening attentively and responding audibly can help a struggling sermon to soar, while a congregation that does not respond or refuses to listen can fatally wound an otherwise powerful proclamation of the gospel.

Finally, we can explore how worship makes people a part of the church, both consciously and unconsciously. Consider the ways worship both forms and reflects the congregation. For example, watching the way young children, who do not understand content, participate in worship (or "play church") provides important clues in this regard.

Those who participate are so important that, in White's scheme, *people* stand at the center of the seven categories and relate to both the circumstances of worship (piety, time, and place) and the acts of worship (prayer, preaching, music). People are key to understanding worship.

Piety

Spirituality or *piety* concerns the ways people relate to God and to each other. Do people approach God as intimate and knowable or as transcendent and mysterious? Do people regard themselves and others as the apple of God's eye or as sinners deserving only God's wrath?[10] The most important question about piety for preaching is whether people—preachers and listeners—really expect God to speak in and through the sermon. Is preaching a word from God or words about God?

A congregation's piety is hard to assess for three reasons. First, piety is very subjective. What some congregations regard as proper others dismiss as rigid and still others as irreverent. Overt displays of piety, such as crossing oneself and genuflecting or saying amen during a sermon, are expected in some congregations, tolerated in others, and negatively sanctioned in still others. My family regularly reminds me that voicing approval during sermons, which my preaching students appreciate in the classroom and seminary chapel, draws disbelieving stares in many of the congregations where we worship.

A second reason piety is difficult to assess is that crosscurrents of different pieties operate within the same congregation. For example, while some in a congregation regard the Lord's Supper as a foretaste of the resurrected life and desire to receive it often, others, who regard the Lord's Supper solely in terms of forgiveness, do not understand themselves sinning enough to warrant frequent celebration. The piety reflected in how frequently Holy Communion is part of worship might be a compromise among several pieties rather than an expression of the congregation's piety.

The third reason that a congregation's piety is difficult to analyze is that piety can change over time, for example, from penitential to resurrection focused. I once preached in a congregation that I experienced as somber and inflexible; worship leaders were afraid of making mistakes and doing anything wrong, and worshipers were critical. Years later, I was invited to return and found a different spirit. People smiled and were gracious; worship leaders were relaxed and joyful. Even the music was more uplifting. Though it is challenging, piety deserves examination, because preaching and worship are always shaded in the direction of someone's piety—the minister's, the congregation's, or some group's within the congregation.

Time

As in all of life's activities, what people do in worship is heavily conditioned by the *time* when it occurs. I am frequently asked how long sermons should be. In other words, how should sermons fit in time? Rather than offering a number of minutes, I respond that a sermon or worship service's location in time strongly influences both the expectations worshipers bring and the interpretations they assign. Some congregations worship, some ministers preach, and some parishioners listen for as long as the Spirit leads them; other congregations are constrained to fit the entire service within a well-established time limit, such as an hour. I have discovered that when sermons are too short for too many weeks, parishioners become uncomfortable and question whether the preacher is devoting adequate time to sermon preparation.

In addition to how much time they take, some sermons and worship services derive meaning from how often they occur. Some sermons and worship services are significant because, rather than being weekly events, they only occur occasionally. For marginal Christians, for example, the points at which worship marks significant life passages—baptism, marriage, and burial—are their only contacts with the church. For these millions of Christians, baptisms, weddings, and funerals are the church's most important services. For millions more Christians, annual festivals, particularly Christmas and Easter, are their most important contact with the church. For many practicing Christians, a week without worship feels incomplete or abnormal. In some congregations, worship is governed by a liturgical calendar, the church's way of keeping time. In these contexts, festivals and seasons provide a frame of reference for interpreting Scripture and preaching, so that the congregation hears the gospel from different perspectives and with different emphases. In other congregations, worship is governed by calendars more culturally connected to people's lives.

Lucy Lind Hogan, professor of preaching and worship at Wesley Theological Seminary in Washington, D.C., encourages preachers to consider time in their preaching by holding the past, present, and future in a divine tension or balance.[11] Sermons ought to balance recalling God's mighty deeds of the past, caring for our neighbors in the present, and keeping before us the knowledge that our lives and our futures are in God's powerful and loving hands. In this way, preaching will address the full story of salvation— formation and teaching, mission and Christian responsibility to the world today, and God's future, the *eschaton*.

Because time is so important to a congregation's worship, the ways in which the rhythms of various cycles both reflect and shape individuals and the community must be taken into account. Exploring the daily, weekly, annual, liturgical, programmatic, secular, and lifetime calendars at work in the congregation can reveal the influence of time on worship.

Place

The *place* where anything happens shapes its meaning. Everyone from politicians declaring their intention to run for office to couples declaring their intention to marry carefully weighs the best place to make their announcement. So too, the place where congregations worship reflects and influences what happens there. For example, the space where preaching occurs forms preacher and congregation and reflects who they are in ways beyond sermon content. When people can see each other during the sermon, they experience preaching as a community gathering. When the church grows dark as a spotlight floods the preacher, preaching becomes individuals watching a performance.

An analysis of a congregation's worship considers the layout of the worship space, the visual accompaniments of worship, and the way sounds behave during worship. First, we can examine the relationship of the basic spaces for worship: gathering, movement, congregational, choir, baptismal, and altar. The way all these spaces relate to each other and to what many consider the four focal points of worship (pulpit, font, altar, and seating for worship leaders) are important indicators of how things work in worship. Does the pulpit or the altar dominate? Are the people arranged in a shoebox-shaped nave away from the action, or do they encircle it?

The design of the four focal points or liturgical centers—pulpit, font, altar, and seating for worship leaders—tells much about the importance accorded to what happens at them. Is the baptismal font a small wooden stand with a bowl on top that gets tucked away in a corner, or a limestone monument that is anchored into the floor? How does the pulpit influence preaching? While a highly elevated, canopied pulpit may be the best acoustically and may afford the word of God a prominent place, for many people such a pulpit may also symbolize a hierarchical church, domination by the clergy, and the removal of the word of God from the people. While some congregations love it when the preacher leaves the pulpit to stand among the people, other congregations feel the preacher has abandoned the place associated with and dedicated to God's word and its corresponding authority to offer opinions and invade their personal space.

Both liturgical art and acoustics also contribute to the worship space. What ambiance does liturgical art create? Does the space make preaching sound powerful and grand or warm and intimate? Does the space lend itself toward vocal expression or clear articulation, so that the congregation hears every word without difficulty? Does preaching sound natural or artificial? Considerations of the worship space include questions concerning what the place indicates about worship priorities and how the place affects worship practices and participation.

Prayer

Turning from the circumstances of worship to the activities of worship, a congregation can better understand itself as a faith community by considering both the form and the leadership of *prayer*. Examining the form of a congregation's prayer reveals how the ministers and people speak to God. Prayer might be fixed in printed books or free and open to local diversity. Congregational prayer can be prepared in advance of worship or left to the spontaneous prompting of the Holy Spirit. The congregation might pray in everyday speech, in elevated prose, or in sacral language from the Elizabethan era. In addition to the ways prayers are crafted, the mechanisms used and the degree to which individual prayers and weekday prayer services relate to the Sunday gathering of the whole community also indicate how the faith community understands its life together.

The leadership of prayer, who voices prayer for the community, indicates whether worship is something the clergy does for the people or the congregation does together. Prayer might be a unison act, a solo performance, or something done spontaneously and simultaneously by everyone. Whether and which prayers are led by the clergy and how both lay-led prayer and the prayers of congregation members are incorporated into worship are practices that can be identified and examined.

The prayers that surround the sermon provide important clues to what the preacher and congregation consider the purpose of preaching to be. Some prayers that begin the sermon, such as prayers of illumination, ask for a right understanding of Scripture; others ask that Christ be present. Some prayers speak of individual worshipers, others the congregation as a whole, and still others the congregation in the world. Prayers that conclude the sermon might ask God to do something, ask God to help the congregation do something, or summarize the sermon for the congregation to overhear.

Pastors and parishioners can consider to what extent the prayers in the worship service are a way the congregation responds to the sermon. At one extreme, some congregations consciously approach these prayers, which frequently follow the sermon, as a kind of business meeting where the community sets its agenda in response to God's message for them in the sermon. At the other extreme, the prayers may exhibit no relation to the sermon or even to the congregation. In my experience, this happens when leaders take prayers from a worship resource and do not edit them.

Some congregations and Christian traditions include a specific form of prayer as part of their celebration of sacraments and other rites. Congregations can consider how they understand and enact the prayer said over the water of baptism, the bread and wine of the Lord's Supper, as well as the oil for healing; and how they understand and enact prayers at confirmation, ordination, marriage, and burial. Who voices these prayers? How do individuals and the congregation participate in these rites? To what extent does preaching speak to the sacraments? How does preaching help the congregation understand them? How does preaching prepare the congregation to participate in the sacraments in worship and to connect the sacraments to their lives, the congregation's ministry, and the world?

Preaching

An appreciation of a sermon's worship context leads to examining the ways the elements of the service, such as hymns, prayers, confession, offering, and sacraments, inform and reinforce the message of the sermon. The style of worship, expressed in the language of prayer and Scripture, ritual action, physical environment, and structures of ministry, forms a specific style that influences the style and content of the sermon.

As an indication of the importance of *preaching* to worship, White notes that, in Protestant traditions, at least a third and often more than half of the service is allotted to the sermon. As we will discuss in chapter 3, preaching takes a variety of forms and serves an assortment of purposes. For example, some sermons are intended to introduce the unchurched to Jesus, others to teach Christian doctrine to the faithful. Biblical preaching can be both exegetical and topical. The form and function of preaching vary even among congregations of the same Christian tradition, which, of course, is the subject of this book.

Music

Both the forms of *music* and who performs it are important considerations when examining a congregation's worship. Music might be included in the service as congregational song or as choral music. The role of instrumental music, or prohibitions against it, should be considered. Is service music present or absent? Most important, does music function as an offering to God, as a proclamation by or to the people, or as both?

Hymns sung most frequently (or sung well) provide especially important evidence of the types of piety prevalent in the congregation, because hymns provide people words to express their faith.

Because hymns have the additional power of repetition when they are sung over the course of weeks, seasons, years, and lifetimes, singing hymns is an effective way to teach the faith. Moreover, inasmuch as hymns are different from sermons and most prayers in that lyrics do not change, they provide one of the best sources of theology and can be used effectively as a source of theological statements.

In all this, the concern is, once again, how preaching and music relate in worship. Some observe that, increasingly, music is used to package the sermon's message. Consider how music prepares the congregation to receive and enables the congregation to respond to the sermon's message. Examine the level of coordination between the sermon and the hymns and choral and instrumental music. Do the musical and preaching styles fit? Are the tempos of the sermon and the music congruent? Does the sermon inspire the congregation to sing, and is the sermon hymn selected an appropriate song? Worshipers report that when the preacher and congregational musician study Scripture together as part of their preparation, the worship service exhibits greater power and coherence.

My expectation here is not that congregations will answer every question, assess every decision, or deliberate every detail suggested by these seven categories for analyzing Christian worship. Rather, these characteristics of Christian worship can help congregations move beyond matters of preference, taste, and correctness to discuss their worship more objectively, in order to ask the more significant questions: What does your congregation's worship communicate about God, faith, the church, and the world? Is this, in fact, what you intend to proclaim?

Worship and Mission

Sometimes pastors and parishioners get so involved in discussing worship and preaching that they forget that the worship service, of which the sermon is a part, is not intended to be either an end in itself or a congregation's only experience of and response to the gospel. One way or another, the church intends and expects that its worship and preaching will make a difference in the world. Put another way, the church expects that its worship and preaching will make the world different, better, more in keeping with God's intention for creation. Today the question of how worship and preaching make the world different, or the relationship between worship and mission, is a primary concern of all expressions of the church. Both at home and throughout the world, the church faces a mission situation unlike anything it has seen since the Peace of Constantine, seventeen hundred years ago. From a missional perspective, the relationship of worship and mission is key to experiencing and expressing the faith in ways appropriate to endemic cultures in parts of the world that historically received patterns of worship from European and North American missionaries, who brought their own worldviews and cultural assumptions. The relationship of worship and mission is also important as the church responds to a postmodern and post-Christian culture in the West, because the worldview that shaped Christian worship is passing away in many places.

Those who lead and study both the church's mission and the church's worship recognize that congregational worship forms and nourishes individual Christians and the mission and ministry of communities of faith in powerful ways. John D. Witvliet, Director of the Calvin Institute of Christian Worship and editor of the Alban Institute's Vital Worship, Healthy Congregations series, describes Christianity as "a 'first-person plural religion,' where communal worship, service, fellowship, and learning are indispensable for grounding and forming individual faith" and the congregation as "the cradle of Christian faith." Witvliet asserts that Christianity in North America depends upon "healthy, spiritually nourishing, well-functioning congregations."[12] Worship is so integral to mission that congregations interested in being "healthy, spiritually nourishing, [and] well-functioning" eventually find themselves reflecting on and reconsidering their worship.

Thomas H. Schattauer, professor of worship at Wartburg Theological Seminary in Dubuque, Iowa, suggests three possible approaches to understanding how Christian worship forms and nourishes the church for mission.[13] I have developed three metaphors, all features of the earth—a mountain, a plain, and a river— to further characterize worship in Schattauer's three approaches.

Figure 2.2. Ways to Characterize the Relationship of
Worship and Mission in a Congregation

All three images are rich in biblical allusions, suggesting that,
though congregations may understand and approach the relationship of worship and mission differently, God acts in and through
all three approaches.

Mountain

In the Bible, a mountain is a place where people meet God and significant things happen. God spared Abraham from sacrificing Isaac
on Mount Moriah. God appears to Moses on Mount Sinai. Mount
Carmel is the site of the contest between Elijah and the prophets
of Baal, and Mount Horeb is where Elijah heard God's still, small
voice. The "mountain of the Lord" will rise up as the place from
which God's word goes forth to all people and to which the whole
world will be drawn. On this mountain, God will prepare the great
feast at the end of time. Mountains provide the setting for Jesus's
preaching, transfiguration, and ascension.

Like a mountain, worship in Schattauer's first approach is a
place we go to meet God. We encounter God in worship inside the
church, and mission occurs outside the church—when the gospel is
proclaimed to those who have not heard or received it or when the
neighbor is served in acts of justice and love. On the mountain that
is worship, the Christian and the congregation access God's grace
and are spiritually empowered to take up the church's mission in

the world; God's grace, experienced and received in worship, propels individual and community to both proclaim the gospel and love and serve the neighbor. Christians might imagine themselves as part of the seventy Jesus appointed and sent on ahead of him in pairs to every town and place where Jesus intended to go, and who returned to Jesus filled with joy, having exercised great authority in Jesus's name.[14] Sustained by grace in life before God and life among God's people, Christians and the congregation as a whole go out as proclaimers and doers of the gospel. They return to worship, perhaps with a few more people gathered by their witness, where they are recharged by God's grace, and the process begins again. Coming to church is coming into Jesus's presence. Worship is designed to sustain, equip, and commission Christians for Christ's work in the world.

Plain

In Scripture, God comes to and addresses God's people on the plain or level place. Isaiah describes the coming of the Lord on a level place, where valleys are lifted up, hills made low, uneven ground made level, and rough places smoothed into a plain. Moses speaks the words that God commanded him to speak to all Israel on the plain. In Luke, Jesus comes down from the mountain and stands on a level place to speak to a crowd of his disciples and a great multitude of people, leading some to refer to this portion of Luke's Gospel as the "Sermon on the Plain."[15] The psalms describe the way of the righteous or the way of the Lord as a level path or level ground.

In Schattauer's second approach, the church's mission—proclaiming the gospel and loving the neighbor—becomes the purpose of the church's worship. The worship service becomes the *plain*, where God comes and speaks to the people, presenting either the gospel to the unchurched and irreligious or a program for serving the neighbor, often through political or social action. The congregation makes the visitor or neighbor its priority on Sunday morning. Echoing Jesus's parable of the great dinner,[16] the congregation expends great energy to bring the unchurched through the church door, to make them feel welcome, and to meet their needs. Worship is reshaped to be level ground, where the unchurched feel at home and comfortable. On this plain the church takes up the tasks of mission, where mission is defined as evangelical outreach, social transformation, or both. Perhaps Jesus's own Sermon on the Plain is an example of this approach to the relationship of worship and mission. Here, Jesus comes down from the mountain, stands on a level place with a great multitude of people, all looking to have their needs met, and teaches them about the reign of God. Examples of this approach to worship and mission include the church growth movement and both liberal and conservative congregations that seek to orient worship to specific social and political goals.

River

In Scripture, flowing water, such as a river, represents God's initiative and activity in human history and in the world. At creation, a stream arose from the earth before the Garden of Eden was made. God recreated the world through the waters of the flood, and created a holy people, first through the waters of the Red Sea and then through the waters of baptism. Israel, Elijah, and Jesus all passed through the river Jordan. Water flowed from Jesus's side after his death on the cross. Isaiah describes God's salvation as burning sand becoming pools, and the thirsty ground springs of water; God will make waters in the wilderness and rivers in the desert. In the new Jerusalem, "the river of the water of life, bright as crystal, [flows] from the throne of God and of the Lamb through the middle of the street of the city. On either side of the river is the tree of life with its twelve kinds of fruit, producing its fruit each month; and the leaves of the tree are for the healing of the nations."[17]

In Schattauer's third approach, both worship and mission are currents in the *river* of God's salvation and recreation. Neither are primarily activities of the church or the Christian. This approach understands "the life and history of Israel, the saving work of Jesus, and the mission of the early church as these events are proclaimed in Scripture to be connected to one another and to the

church's worship . . . as the single, continuing story of God's saving activity in Jesus Christ."[18] God's work of salvation, recorded
in Scripture and accomplished in Christ, continues to our day in
the church's worship. Perhaps the most striking biblical example
of this approach to worship and mission is Paul's teaching that
the people of Israel were baptized into Christ when they passed
through the sea and that baptism unites us to Christ's death and
resurrection.[19] The participation of the Christian and the congregation are like stones carried along in the river of God's gracious
work of salvation. We can cooperate with the river's current or be
indifferent to or even attempt to resist it, but God's work of salvation and renewal continues nevertheless. The church witnesses to
and is drawn into God's own purpose of reconciling the world to
God's own self. Worship is the way God gathers people to witness
to and participate in God's work of reconciliation. The judgment
and mercy of God, proclaimed and enacted in worship, signify
God's ultimate judgment and mercy for the world. In this way,
God's people worshiping in the midst of the world enact and signify God's own mission for the life of the world. The worshiping
congregation is the location where God carries out God's mission.
Reflecting on the historic order for Holy Communion as the Divine Liturgy gives us insight into this approach to worship and
mission, as do charismatic and Pentecostal worship. Many regard
these expressions of worship more as God's activity than as the
people's. More concretely, the Lord's Supper might be understood
as God modeling and enacting the divine will for food distribution
in the world; that is, in God's reign, food will be distributed in the
world as the Eucharist is distributed in the church—everyone gets
an equal share so that all are fed.

However a congregation understands and approaches the relationship of worship and mission, the sermon and Sunday service
are the primary means by which the Spirit leads Christians and
congregations to live and serve as Christ's presence in the world. As
such, preaching and the assumptions that surround it exert great
influence on a congregation's understanding and implementation
of its overall mission and ministry. But what aim ought the sermon
serve? In the next chapter, we consider the purposes of preaching.

Questions for Discussion

- What makes a worship service worshipful for you? What is the most meaningful or important part of worship for you?
- If someone asked you to describe the people in your congregation (or worship service), what three words would you use?
- What is your favorite hymn? What does that hymn suggest about how you understand your relationship with God?
- What does your congregation's worship space suggest is most important about worship and being Christian?
- How do your personal prayers connect to the prayers of your congregation?
- Do you understand the relationship of worship and mission as a mountain, plain, river, or something else? Explain.

Chapter Three

What Is a Sermon?

It's a typical Sunday at St. Ambrose Church. Pastor Mark stands at the church door, greeting parishioners after the service. "Good sermon," people say. "I'm glad you found it meaningful," the preacher responds, clueless as to what the churchgoers mean by *good*. Sitting in the last pew, Connie sighs while listening as people compliment the preacher, for, though everyone else praises the pastor's preaching, the sermon did not speak to Connie. The scene is not unique to St. Ambrose Church but plays out each Sunday in congregations across the country and around the world. The sermon speaks to some but not to others. How can this be?

What is a sermon? People decide that a sermon is *good* in large part based on their expectations of what the form, content, and delivery of a sermon ought to be. We tend to think that we all know what a sermon is. The dictionary definition of a sermon, "a talk on a religious or moral subject, especially one given during a church service," suggests that a sermon is something the minister preaches and the congregation listens to or observes. Yet, many of the church's most important "sermons" are preached outside of worship by baptized Christians who, for example, share the faith with their children, allow the gospel to guide their business dealings, and work for justice and peace in the various arenas of their lives. In these and many other ways, Christians proclaim the gospel to people and in places that preachers in pulpits may never reach. Teresa L. Fry Brown, who teaches preaching at Candler School of Theology in Atlanta, writes: "All persons have authority to proclaim, to tell others about the prophecy, birth, life, ministry, death, resurrection, and second coming of Jesus Christ. The *kairos* or *fullness of time* is God's time, place, and appointed person(s) that occur to actualize God's promise."[1] The Sunday sermon, which is the subject of this chapter, is but a part of the church's proclamation of the gospel and frequently not the most important part.

I increasingly imagine the church as a stadium in which an important contest is taking place. The stands are filled with the people of the world—family, friends, neighbors, coworkers, fellow citizens, people of other cultures, people of other faiths, people of no faith—who watch as the proclaimers of the gospel of Jesus Christ compete with all those forces opposed to God's will and work in the world. I imagine that contest to be a school football game. The Christian team that takes the field is made up of the people in the pew; like any school team, the players are not professionals, though they are certainly talented and play with heart. Though the professionals—the clergy—sometimes play quarterback, for the really big plays they are on the sidelines coaching. Other expressions of the church, such as bishops and church bureaucrats, are in the press box or a blimp, offering a more panoramic perspective. Seminary professors like me are on a practice field next door to the stadium, training those who are to coach God's people in the big games of this ongoing competition.

From this perspective, the purpose of the Sunday sermon is to inspire, equip, and empower the congregation to proclaim the gospel in the world. Preacher and author Barbara Brown Taylor describes the purpose of the Sunday sermon as inviting the congregation to see the world as the realm of God's activity and to make connections between the Christian faith and their lives in the same way they hear them made from the pulpit, until they become preachers themselves. Taylor writes: "Preaching is not something an ordained minister does for fifteen minutes on Sundays, but what the whole congregation does all week long; it is a way of approaching the world, and of gleaning God's presence there."[2]

In carrying out this purpose, the Sunday sermon takes a wide variety of forms and serves an assortment of functions. Preaching can focus on bringing unbelievers to Christ or the unchurched into the congregation. Or, preaching might be a doctrinal lesson for the faithful. The church preaches to bear witness to the good news of Christ, to ensure that the faithful will not forget the details of their

Figure 3.1. What Is a Sermon?

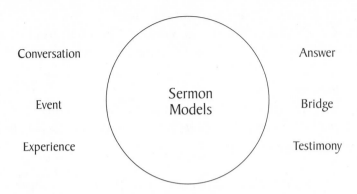

Conversation   Answer

Event   Sermon   Bridge
                         Models

Experience   Testimony

faith, to help people make sense of their lives in light of the gospel, to shape the congregation's life together, to interpret Scripture, to pronounce divine judgment, and to assure people of God's love. Preaching can be highly exegetical, interpreting the meaning of a biblical text for contemporary life, or a sermon can begin with a topic of human concern and apply biblical insights to it. Preaching can be extremely formal or highly conversational, intellectual or emotional, experiential or theoretical. Regardless of what the sermon is and does, the preacher will both receive the compliment at the church door and overhear the sigh in the last pew.

In this chapter, I offer six possible responses to the question, What is a sermon? A sermon might be (1) an *answer*, (2) an *event*, (3) an *experience*, (4) a *bridge*, (5) a *testimony*, and (6) a *conversation*. This is by no means an exhaustive list. For example, in *The Purposes of Preaching*, a wonderful collection of essays, "leading scholars in the field of homiletics, all of them powerful preachers," describe the purposes of preaching in North America in the late 20th and early 21st centuries.[3] Their list of the purposes of preaching includes the following:

- interpreting life theologically through conversation;
- building up the community of faith in practices of discipleship;
- opening people to God's ongoing and unfolding work in the world revealed in Jesus Christ;

- presenting the acknowledged word of God in such a way that the listener or observer senses the impulse of change or conversion in his or her own life;
- forming Christians for and calling Christians to mission;
- speaking what cannot be spoken, empowering and being silenced by those who have little voice, and even less power;
- disrupting life to create a space in which the Holy Spirit can lead the community to rethink, revisit, and receive; and
- communicating faith.

I am grateful for these colleagues' descriptions of the purposes of preaching and draw upon them in my own reflections in this chapter.

When I say that the Sunday sermon might be an *answer*, an *event*, an *experience*, a *bridge*, a *testimony*, and a *conversation*, I understand these responses as models of sermons. By *sermon model*, I intend more than the sermon's form or shape. Though some contend that the unchanging gospel fits into any package, communication theory suggests that the container forms and even changes its contents. For me, a *sermon model* includes (1) the place and interpretation of Scripture, (2) the ways the gospel is formulated and articulated, (3) how the sermon is crafted and delivered, and (4) the way the preacher and listeners participate in the sermon. I therefore use these four characteristics to describe each of the six sermon models.

Sermon as Answer

At St. Ambrose Church, Drew views the sermon as an *answer* to his questions. In Mark's Gospel, Jesus preaches in the temple during Passover, various people bring questions to him, and Jesus gives them answers. Jesus fit their questions into his preaching and teaching ministry. Jesus was glad to take up the questions of the day and discuss them. Mark indicates that Jesus answered several questions in the temple—regarding the lawfulness of paying taxes to Caesar, whether the dead are raised up to eternal life, the most important commandment, and how the Messiah can be David's son.[4]

Those who desire the sermon to be an answer understand the truth of the gospel and the way Christians live to be contained in the written pages of the Bible: we can open the Bible and find the answers we need. Good preaching is true to the Bible, which often means that the connection between Scripture and sermon is obvious. Taken to the extreme, people who consider the sermon an answer want assurance that the words of the Bible and the words of the preacher are, syllable for syllable, God's words. To be honest, all Christians and all congregations have moments when we earnestly desire such certainty and clarity. When tragedy strikes or we face a tough decision, we want God through the preacher to give us such an answer. We approach passages from Scripture with our questions and reduce them to the answers they provide, the lessons they teach, and the doctrines they illuminate. The truth of the gospel is objective, universal, and often propositional. Paul offers one such proposition: "For we hold that a person is justified by faith apart from works prescribed by the law."[5]

The problem, of course, is that often when Jesus's answers are clear and straightforward, they are hard for us to hear and accept. We ask, "What does Jesus expect of disciples?" In the Sermon to the Disciples, Jesus tells us that disciples are to proclaim good news; are to give without expecting payment; and are not to take money, a bag, or even a change of clothes. When Jesus began to openly teach the disciples that he must undergo great suffering, be rejected, be killed, and after three days rise again, Peter took Jesus aside and began to rebuke him.[6]

When we understand the sermon as an answer, the goal of preaching is persuasion, to get the congregation, aided by grace or the Spirit, to accept, assent to, or agree with a truth claim about God and Christ by an act of will. The sermon tells people what they should believe and why they should believe it. This kind of preaching is very effective at eliciting intellectual assent to a particular doctrinal formulation, challenging heresy, and convincing people that it is Christian to act a certain way.

In this approach to preaching, the preacher is often regarded as a teacher, an authority in Scripture and the things of God who dispenses information to the congregation. The congregation is student or recipient. The preacher wants the congregation to understand and accept some insight or belief, and his or her task is to inform and persuade. The preacher teaches, explaining the Bible and instructing the congregation in Christian doctrine and its connection to life. The preacher defines, transmits, informs, convinces, explains, and communicates gospel truth.[7] The preacher also exhorts the congregation to agree with the gospel truth and live accordingly. The language of the sermon is clear, accurate, precise, and convincing. Sermons are structured to communicate a proposition or a central idea. For example, the preacher might identify a current issue or a question to which the gospel provides an answer or offer an exposition of the relevance and significance of a biblical text for today's world. Stories and experience might be used to illustrate the point; however, for people like Drew, a story sermon without an explicit moral or point simply will not suffice.

Traditionally, when the aim of the sermon is to provide an answer, preaching and Scripture tend to dominate the worship service. The supremacy of God's word and preaching is often reflected in the worship space, where the pulpit is really the only focal point. Worship might be thought of as the classroom in which the lesson of the sermon takes place. People participate in worship individually and approach God intellectually. Thus, worship tends to be cognitive and content centered; elements in worship, such as creed, confession, and hymns, properly express and reinforce the truth of the gospel. Technology, such as PowerPoint, might be effectively used to summarize and visually present information. People who want to feel something in worship are likely to be disappointed. People often participate in worship that includes this type of sermon passively; the congregation sits below while the preacher stands above them declaring absolute truth. In this traditional approach, people who want to feel something in worship are likely to be disappointed. A more recent form of worship in which the sermon functions as an answer is joyful and participatory, however. Energetic and emotional praise music prepares the congregation to receive the sermon and connects the congregation to the preacher. The worship service appeals to people's hearts so the sermon can speak to their minds. Regardless of the form of worship, having received and assented to the correct formulation of the Christian faith in worship, the congregation is prepared to carry out its mission of proclaiming the truth of the gospel in the world. Using the images for the relationship between worship and mission discussed in chapter 2, worship is most like a mountain.

Sermon as Event

Audrey understands the sermon as an *event* in which God speaks a word of promise to God's people as the essential core of the gospel is proclaimed. The word *redemption* might describe the purpose of this event. Charles Campbell in *The Purposes of Preaching* suggests that preaching is "a word that enables the people of God to step into the freedom from the powers of death given through Jesus's life, death and resurrection."[8] In and through preaching, God brings people from death to new life; God releases people from bondage and empowers them to step out of the tomb and live the new life exemplified and inaugurated by Jesus. In the Gospels, Jesus speaks words that give people freedom and new life. For example, Jesus says to the thief on the cross, "Truly I tell you, today you will be with me in Paradise." Jesus cries out, "Lazarus, come out!" and the dead man comes out of the tomb.[9]

Christians like Audrey, who understand the sermon as an event, hold that God communicates God's very self to humanity through events in time and space, most notably the event of the life, death, and resurrection of Jesus Christ. Scripture contains the recorded stories of the events of God, which are models or paradigms or prototypes of how God has related and continues to relate to God's people and the world. The transforming images and messages contained in Scripture, especially those involving Jesus, are the key to naming and understanding what God is doing and how we are to live. Through telling and retelling incidents of God's saving self-revelation, particularly in Christ, God brings about saving faith, holy living, and eternal life. This understanding of Scripture and preaching assumes that human words communicate God's word. In fact, the apostolic word and, subsequently, the preached word have the same authority and power as the word of God or Jesus. As the word of God is mediated through Christ, so God spoke through prophets and speaks through preachers when the gospel is proclaimed. Words, then, are more than tools used to communicate a message. They are the agents of God's self-disclosure and immediacy. As such, words have the effect they proclaim. For example, words of forgiveness do forgive. Words of healing do heal. Words of condemnation do condemn. For, as Paul declares, "we proclaim Christ crucified . . . Christ the power of God and the wisdom of God."[10] This word from God causes the hearers to respond in faith.

The content of preaching as an event is the essential gospel, "the good news of Jesus Christ entrusted to the preacher through Scripture,"[11] as God's saving activity today. In other words, the preacher proclaims the promise of God revealed and enacted in the life, death, and resurrection of Jesus Christ and the difference that promise makes for our lives and for the world today. The preacher proclaims the gospel to listeners to whom he or she has been sent, who may be experiencing questions, doubts, and thoughts that are opposite God's plan and promise of life. In order to proclaim the gospel promise in ways that help the congregation, the preacher seeks to be aware of and respond to people's needs; the preacher may even diagnose those needs and attempt to respond to them with the particular parts of the gospel message that people need at the moment and can receive amid the pain and clutter of their lives. Even when these realities may not be known to the preacher, they are known to God. When the gospel is preached, God permeates the personal or communal barriers, changing lack of faith, doubting faith, or struggling faith through God's promise, forgiveness, acceptance, and chance to begin again. Exhortation therefore flows from the proclamation of the gospel. In this way, preaching attempts to open people to God before attempting to get people to do anything else. "In some theological traditions, openness is regarded as the one thing human beings have to offer God; in others, God supplies even this. . . . To preach Jesus Christ is to allow God's word to work through one's personality and expressiveness in such a way that both preacher and congregation are opened."[12]

Stated another way, preaching disrupts life to create a space in which the Holy Spirit can work, a space in which the community can rethink, revisit priorities, or receive.[13]

The form of the sermon should be congruent with the promise from God it seeks to proclaim; the sermon's form is often to be found in the passage of Scripture on which the sermon is based. For example, rather than providing a definite interpretation, a sermon based on one of Jesus's parables would itself be parabolic as it invites the hearers to see the world from God's perspective.

In this model of preaching, the preacher is a messenger, speaking to the people for God and to God for the people. The messenger's task is to clearly and accurately announce God's message, the promise of the gospel. As God's messenger, the preacher stands as an authority figure who brings the gospel formulation or reformulation to the hearers. At the same time, the preacher is part of the congregation, so that she or he can announce the good news these people need to receive. While the preacher's personality, character, experiences, and relationships with the hearers are important, they are secondary to the person and authority of Christ. Therefore, rather than being ends in themselves, the preacher's words, deeds, and inner experience serve the gospel by being as congruent as possible with the person and promise of the One on whose behalf the preacher speaks. Preaching the gospel in a meaningful way emphasizes the congregation, rather than the preacher. The congregation brings its realities, waits expectantly to receive a word from God, and responds to that word in faith and new life. Those who consider preaching as an event tend to regard the congregation as a gathering of individuals. The goal is often that each individual worshiper has a personal encounter with Christ.

Some argue that expecting every sermon to be an event in which God speaks a word of promise is not reasonable; this high expectation causes both preachers and congregants to go away from the sermon feeling disappointed because, for whatever reason, the Spirit did not show up. A second concern about preaching as an event is the difficulty of translating the gospel into a word of promise that means something to particular people on a specific occasion. Unable to find the words and committed to preaching the gospel, preachers might reduce their proclamation of the gospel to a formula or proposition, or simply mouth traditional language. People worry that the preacher will alter, reinvent, add to, evaluate, or water down either the grace or the claim of the gospel. Some worry that people may mistake the preacher's voice for the voice of God; should this happen, the pastoral relationship, and even the congregation, might be characterized by hierarchy and distance between the preacher and the people. Yet another concern is that this approach to preaching may become so focused on the individual worshiper, in order to facilitate a personal encounter with Christ, that it neglects speaking to the congregation as a community of faith and relating the gospel to the world. Alternatively, people who do not feel individually addressed in the sermon may conclude that God has nothing to say to them.

At its best, preaching as an event results in worshipers communing both with God and with the worshiping congregation. The proclamation of the gospel is the basis of worship. Worship is where God speaks to God's people. The worship service provides other means by which God addresses the congregation through sight, sound, touch, taste, and movement and by which the people respond to God in faith, praise, thanksgiving, and commitment. Music and technology might be enlisted for this purpose. Responding in faith, the congregation carries out its mission, announcing to the world the word from the Lord it received in worship and doing what God calls it to do. This worship functions as a mountain, perhaps as a river, but not so much as a plain.

Sermon as Experience

Connie understands the sermon as an *experience* of Christ, grace, forgiveness, or love that transforms the hearers. Connie desires preaching that helps people feel closer to God, so they are inspired to grow in faith and love. Christians like Connie are not as interested in hearing the gospel as in feeling the presence of God. They want to be touched, moved, excited, and empowered by God. They want preaching to uplift, empower, and motivate them. Like the Greeks who approached Philip at the festival of the Passover, these Christians want to see Jesus rather than understand who Jesus is.

The aim of this kind of preaching is to provide an experience of God's presence that transforms individuals and the congregation. Throughout the Gospels, Jesus's preaching is paired with such experiences—healing, multiplying loaves and fish, cleansing the temple. Today, elements of the worship service, such as music, technology, architecture, and sacraments, provide such pairings. More important than these pairings, Jesus's preaching is itself an occasion on which his hearers experience God—sowing seed, finding a pearl buried in a field, and traveling from Jerusalem to Jericho.

In this approach to preaching, speaking the content of the gospel is less important than helping people feel Christ's presence, love, and power. Rather than proclaiming a word from God, the aim of the sermon is creating an experience that changes the worshipers' values, worldview, or reality. Often, this kind of preaching is characterized by storytelling and evocative and poetic language. Fans of this approach to preaching remind other churchgoers that narrative and imaginative language are traits of the Bible and the Christian faith. Human beings like stories, live out of stories, remember and dream in stories, determine their values in stories. Human beings construct reality and determine their place in it using images and stories.

To create an experience, Scripture is interpreted not so much for its original meaning or objective truth but for its power to shape meaning in the lives of the preacher, individual listeners, and the community of faith. The Bible is less a document to be studied and more a story to be told. The gospel proclamation takes the form of a narration of events—Jesus's life, death, and resurrection—that people can enter into, rather than a system of doctrine. Scripture stimulates the church's imagination and helps the faithful see life in new ways, as people identify with a biblical character and connect faith with their routine experience.

Rather than a teacher, the preacher is a storyteller. The preacher has greater responsibility for employing the sermon's form, language, and delivery to provide an experience of God. The preacher uses stories as illustrations, shapes sermons as stories, and may even build in ambiguity, as Jesus did in the parables. Rather than providing accuracy or clarity, language is used to evoke a change in the human situation. Words and images are used to change people's perceptions, worldviews, and values because new language creates a new reality. More than describing, words possess the power to create an emotional experience in the hearers. The preacher stands under the word of God with congregation members, who bear greater responsibility for creating the experience by their participation in preaching. The congregation cannot be passive but must participate in creating the world of the story. The hearers fill in missing details, draw their own conclusions, and discover how they will carry the experience into their own faith and life. Critics of this approach to preaching warn that experience may so overshadow substance that preaching is reduced to emotionalism without content, "fluff with no stuff," so that people leave worship feeling good but with nothing to sustain their life of faith.

For those who value preaching as an experience, the church is the community gathered by God's story that participates in and finishes God's story. The worship service is sensory and emotive; the worship leader may invite people to feel a certain way as they listen to a song or pray. The church's mission is to do everything it can to bring people into worship, so that they can experience God. Thus, the connection between worship and mission is a plain.

Sermon as Bridge

Pastor Mark thinks of the sermon as a *bridge* that connects the congregation to the saving acts of God, recorded in the Bible, as they are celebrated and enacted in worship, especially through water, word, bread, and wine. This model of the sermon proclaims that God acts in the forms and actions of Christian worship, particularly baptism and the Lord's Supper, in the same way that God acted in the Bible—to give faith, forgiveness, new life, and a vocation or calling. Preaching draws the hearers into God's saving activity in worship, moving the congregation to enter spiritually and intellectually into God's unfolding work in worship and the world. The goal of this preaching is to enlighten and deepen the hearers' understanding and experience of Christian worship, as God's way of leading them to live in the different, new dimension that is the

Christian life. Jesus's explanation of washing his disciples' feet is one example of such a bridge; Jesus also preached about prayer, fasting, offering, and the Eucharist.[14]

This model of preaching also holds that God acts to give faith and new life when the gospel is proclaimed in preaching and enacted in worship. Through preaching, God leads Christians to see their lives and the world with the eyes of faith, using the worship in which they participate as their lens. In this way, God moves people to see beyond the temporal to the eternal, beyond the realities of this world to the reality of God's kingdom. More than intellectual assent, faith is entering into a new world and a new way of life. Critics worry that this approach to preaching may so privilege worship that other dimensions of Christian faith and life are lost.

Preaching that is a bridge is based on a solid understanding of the history, structure, and theology of worship, which are found in the Bible. Scripture is the interpretive key, because it provides both the meaning of worship and the sacraments and the images used to explain them. Christian history, particularly the biblical narrative of salvation, continues to the present and the future. Christ's life, death, and resurrection stand at the center of salvation history. Christ's saving work was prefigured and foretold in the Old Testament, was recorded in the Gospels, was extended in the apostolic church, and continues until today in the preaching and worship of the church. Using biblical stories and images, the preacher guides particular people into a deeper experience, understanding, and appreciation of the specific rites in which they have participated. The preacher draws upon the hearers' own experience in order to move the hearers from focusing on images, words, and actions to comprehending their significance for Christian faith and their implications for Christian life. Preaching invites particular people into a deeper experience, understanding, and appreciation of the specific rites in which they have participated and the difference participating in these rites makes in real life. Again, critics note that not every passage of Scripture is about worship and imposing this interpretive key will obscure or negate a text's true intent.

When the sermon is a bridge, the preacher functions as a guide, helping the congregation encounter and be encountered by God in their experience of worship. Sermon preparation involves as much prayer and reflection as traditional study. Preachers must understand not only what the church and its theologians teach about worship and the sacraments. Preachers also must understand what they themselves believe about worship and the sacraments. In so doing, they will have something real and important to say about the difference worship and the sacraments make in their lives and in the lives of their listeners, and they will be able to say it concretely.

The form and language of this model of preaching are more associative than discursive, more poetic than philosophical. These sermons are organized as a journey through the rite. Along the way, the preacher addresses the congregation directly in order to bring their experience to mind. The preacher might ask questions, describe actions, and incorporate the words of the worship service into the sermon. Preaching that bridges Scripture and church, worship and mission, explores rather than explains the mystery of God's saving activity. This approach understands that preaching can point to, hint at, and even glimpse this mystery, but preaching cannot define or exhaust its meaning. Thus, preaching as a bridge piles up meanings rather than seeking clear definitions. For example, baptism is tomb and womb, death and resurrection, absolution and new birth. Baptism heals, cleanses, washes away sins, and cancels guilt. This kind of preaching is "both/and" rather than "either/or." Some argue that using images, appealing to all the senses, providing a surplus of meanings, and grounding meaning in experience make this approach to preaching well suited for preaching in a postmodern context.[15] Those who desire clarity and definition find these sermons frustrating.

In this model, the church's mission is to worship. Through preaching and worship, the members of the congregation are formed to view themselves and the world through the lens of Christian worship and to live according to that vision, until that day when the actions of Christian worship and the ways of the world are indistinguishable. Thus, the church's mission is to worship using rites that are worthy of celebrating Christ's life, death, and resurrection and to celebrate those rites worthily. The relationship of worship and mission is a river.

Sermon as Testimony

For Eleanor, what the preacher says is less important than whether the preacher believes what he or she says. For listeners like Eleanor, the preacher functions as a witness, and the sermon is the preacher's *testimony* to faith in Jesus Christ. Anna Carter Florence, who teaches preaching at Columbia Theological Seminary in Decatur, Georgia, states that testimony is not "telling your story" or "using personal illustrations." Testimony is a narration of events and a confession of belief; we tell what we have seen and heard, and we confess what we believe about it. To testify to the gospel is to see and confess glimpses of "the truth in Jesus Christ, the truth that encounters us in concrete human experience, by the grace of God."[16] This testimony does not belong to the witness but proceeds directly from God. Jesus assures the disciples, "When they bring you to trial and hand you over, do not worry beforehand about what you are to say; but say whatever is given you at that time, for it is not you who speak, but the Holy Spirit."[17] Despite this assurance, some worry that the spotlight will shine so bright on the witness that Jesus will be left in the shadows. People who desire an objective proclamation of the gospel that transcends someone's perspective and experience are often disappointed.

Testimony's greatest asset is that it is a practice of the church open to all believers. All Christians can deepen their own faith and the faith of others by passionately witnessing to Christ through the way they live and express their faith.[18] The sermon is a unique form of testimony, because it occurs as part of a worship service and is made in response to both the reading of biblical texts and the context and circumstances of a particular faith community. "The preacher tells what she has seen and heard, in the biblical text and in life, and then confesses what she believes about it."[19] As testimony, the sermon rests on faith rather than proof; its aim is to communicate conviction rather than certainty. Proving whether a sermon is true or false is impossible; one can only believe a sermon or reject it.

The most obvious Christian testimony comes from John the Baptist. In John's Gospel, the Baptizer's testimony is essentially the gospel. But Jesus also testified to the reign of God. In the parables, Jesus used everyday images to portray a new reality, a new world. Jesus also pointed out glimpses of this reality. For example, when the seventy returned and reported that, in Jesus's name, the demons submitted to them, Jesus testified to God's ultimate victory. "I watched Satan fall from heaven like a flash of lightning," Jesus said.[20] Particularly in John's Gospel, Jesus also testified to himself through his works and by interpreting Scripture. Throughout the New Testament, "witnesses testify to what they have seen and heard: a woman at the tomb, a disciple at Pentecost, the risen Lord, the apostle Paul."[21]

Scripture itself is a faithful witness to God's saving activity and claim on life. The Bible does not contain proof of the gospel or facts about the gospel; the Bible testifies to the gospel. For this reason, congregations send preachers to engage the liberating power of God's word in Scripture on their behalf. Rather than being the thing to which the preacher applies Scripture, the community gives Scripture life and meaning, because only the community can elicit a text's specific confession of faith. After encountering God's presence and hearing God's voice, preachers report back to the congregation, testifying to what God is saying and doing. Preachers root themselves so deeply in the biblical text and in the congregational context that they embody God's word.

The relationship of preacher and congregation is that of a witness who has seen and seeks to justify the report and people who have not seen but hear the report and formulate an opinion or belief about that report. Rather than relying on the authority of an office, the preacher claims authority as one of the community who has seen and believed the liberating power of God's Word, then risks proclaiming the truth of the gospel.[22] As a witness, the preacher uses both speech and action; the preacher's entire life participates in this testimony. On the one hand, preachers must be willing to seal their lives to their words, so that how they live is congruent with what they say; on the other hand, preachers are like John the Baptist, who confessed quite openly that he was not the Christ, but that he had come to bear witness to the Christ. Like John, Christian preachers point to Jesus, not to themselves. They bear witness, so that Christ should increase and they should decrease. The congregation appropriates rather than assents to the Christian identity, worldview, and pattern of meaning offered by the witness.

The form and language of the sermon seek to communicate the specific, concrete event the preacher witnessed. To remain true to God's self-disclosure in the cross and resurrection of Jesus Christ, the sermon proclaims God's response to the need of the world in a way that does not coerce or even persuade. Like God, the sermon meets the hearers in their need and confronts the hearers with an alternative reality that makes a claim and prompts (but does not demand) a response. The sermon invites the congregation to enter the witness's world and see it as the witness sees it. At the same time, the sermon creates conditions so that hearers feel safe, valued, and free to choose either not to enter the witness's world or to interpret that world differently. In this way, the testimony sparks, nurtures, focuses, and directs the congregation's mission of testifying to Christ through word and deed in all the world.

Because testimony always calls for judgment, as people must decide whether or not they believe the witness's report, worship can be thought of as a trial in which evidence is presented by the witness of the gospel and by the false witnesses that so fill our lives and the world. Struggle and divergent opinions mark the trial. Competing worldviews and even lives are at stake. At the same time, the worship service prepares the preacher to testify and the hearers to be open to the preacher's testimony as a true and faithful witness to God. Worship functions as a plain, where the unchurched gather to receive the church's witness. Yet, this same trial occurs on the mountain and in the river. In each case, preaching gives the congregation experience testifying to those who need it, so that congregation members will recognize moments when people need testimony, wherever they happen to be, and are ready to testify.

Sermon as Conversation

Fred looks upon the sermon as a *conversation* in which congregation and preacher, together with Scripture, Christian history, doctrine and practice, the greater Christian community, and voices from the world, search for an adequate Christian interpretation of life in all its dimensions, so that the congregation thinks, feels, and acts from the perspective of the gospel.[23] Jesus engaged in this kind of conversation with two women. Jesus talked with a Samaritan woman at a well and a Canaanite woman in the district of Tyre and Sidon.[24]

In the sermon, the preacher facilitates conversation by correlating the claims of Christian tradition from the past or from other communities and locations with the congregation in its present time, context, circumstance, and theological perspective. On behalf of the congregation, the preacher speaks to the contemporary world from the perspective of the gospel and critiques the Christian tradition from the perspective of contemporary insights and experiences. Sermons might reinforce what we hold to be true, prompt us to modify our thoughts and actions, raise questions that we have not previously considered, or introduce us to new possibilities that redirect our thoughts, feelings, and actions. People who come to church seeking a definitive word from God, an explicit proclamation of the gospel, or an experience of the unchanging faith will leave wanting.

The idea of the sermon as a conversation is not about simply a style or form of preaching, such as give-and-take between the preacher and the congregation or turning to a neighbor to discuss something during the worship service. Rather, preachers and congregations engage in ongoing conversation together, in order to come to new insight and understanding because they find the language of faith to be biased, limited, historically conditioned, inextricably bound to the sins of generations and faith communities, and therefore inadequate. As congregations gather around God's word week after week, the gospel fosters and facilitates conversations about core concerns and convictions as the faith community seeks to make sense of life.

Those who regard the sermon as a conversation approach the Bible not as a single book, but as a conversation itself. For these preachers and hearers, the books of the Bible are themselves a conversation among different interpretations of the presence and purposes of God from the perspective of different communities. While these communities certainly share important perspectives, they also put forward different nuances of understanding God and the world. Nevertheless, the Bible has a track record for helping communities of various times and places understand God, themselves, and the world. Rather than serving as the subject matter of sermons, Scripture provides the chosen lens through which God's presence in the world and the implications of that divine presence are viewed by the preacher and offered to the congregation. Together, preacher and congregation explore established interpretations, and the language used to express them, to both uncover the ways they are biased and limited and to discover how the gospel speaks to our world today.

The form of the sermon is a proposal that fosters continued conversation and not a definitive word that silences or resolves conversation. The proposal might be a tentative interpretation of a biblical text or of God's activity. The preacher constructs the sermon as an exploration of a text, doctrine, or situation with the give-and-take among different voices that marks genuine conversation. Through attentive listening to multiple voices in the Bible, Christian tradition, congregation, and beyond, the preacher seeks to help the congregation come to the most adequate interpretation of the presence and purposes of God that it can at the moment. The forms of conversational preaching most suited for this purpose are (1) recharting the process the preacher followed to discover meaning and (2) story or narrative.

In this approach to preaching, the congregation is a roundtable at which preacher and congregants are equal partners in matters of faith and practice. The pulpit is placed on the edge of the community's conversational circle, and the preacher is one voice among many in the congregation's theological, political, historical, ritual, spiritual, and existential conversations.[25] Both preacher and congregation take responsibility for interpreting how the Christian faith is understood and lived both in the church and in the world. Members of the congregation accept responsibility for interpreting faith and life in ways that are accountable to God, one another, the greater church, and the world, particularly those on the margins. Though the preacher speaks in a monologue, members of the congregation participate in the sermon as they would in a conversation with a book or movie. People endeavor to understand and respond

to what they hear; in so doing, they clarify their values and determine courses of action. Preaching urges those of unearned advantage and power to relinquish their privilege and give space for
those who are or feel silenced to speak. In this way, preaching helps
to establish justice and to reclaim what has been silenced in and
stolen from the forgotten and invisible. The authority to preach is
founded on a quality of presence, mutuality, and integrity, all of
which foster an intimate connection that leads to true solidarity
and accompaniment.[26] Thomas G. Long, who teaches preaching at
Emory University's Candler School of Theology, reminds us that,
as attractive as this equalitarian approach sounds, particularly to
preachers, ultimately, the preacher is set apart, called to be the one
who must get up from the roundtable, stand in the pulpit, and
preach.[27]

A single sermon is rarely a preacher and congregation's last
word on a subject. Instead, it is a snapshot of a community's ca-
pacity for discernment at a particular moment. Congregations,
like individuals and households, often mull issues, ideas, feelings,
and decisions over long periods of time. Sermons are in conversation with one another over a season or more of the church's life.[28]
Gathered around God's word week after week, the gospel fosters
and facilitates conversation about the faith community's core concerns and convictions as the faith community seeks to make sense
of life. Week by week, the cumulative effect of sermons contributes
to the congregation's quest to answer core questions. In this way,
the sermon as conversation is an integral expression of the nature
and purpose of the church.

The church's mission as a community of conversation is to
come to a persuasive interpretation of God's purposes for the
world and to mobilize people and resources for participation in
those purposes. Pursuing their ministry and celebrating their gifts,
all congregation members together interpret Scripture. While the
preacher proclaims the gospel in church on Sunday, the congregation preaches in the world during the week. The Sunday sermon
gives birth to the sermons brought into being by individual members of the congregation, who will continue to proclaim the gospel
as the community disperses to dialogue with and act in the world.
Preachers serve as *language teachers* who offer the "vocabulary" of
Christian traditions to their congregations to use to shape, define,

and create reality—that is, to make meaning of God, self, and the world. The real power of the pulpit, therefore, lies in the extended process of modeling how to use the vocabulary of the Christian faith so that the traditional language of ancient Christian communities truly becomes the language of the twenty-first century.[29] Thus preaching unites pastor and people in a shared ministry as the faith community discovers and claims its corporate identity and ways of ordering life.

As the context for the church's conversation, worship creates and supports the relationships of trust, openness, and mutual respect necessary for dialogue in the congregation. Worship is also the regular time when the church pauses to listen to a monologue as part of its continuing conversation. The relationship of worship and mission is most like a river.

In this chapter I presented six models of sermons. I reflected on how Scripture functions in each model, as well as how the gospel is formatted and articulated, the sermon is crafted and delivered, and the ways the preacher and listeners participate. In the next chapter, we consider how people participate in preaching from another perspective, namely how people listen to sermons.

Questions for Discussion

- What do you think is the overall purpose of preaching? Do you agree that the purpose of preaching is to inspire, empower, and equip the congregation to proclaim the gospel in the world?
- Which sermon model best describes your ideal sermon? Which sermon model best describes the kind of sermon you hear most frequently?
- Do you consider the Bible an answer book, a chronicle of God's relationship with humanity, an experience of the Divine, an interpreter of worship, a trusted conversation partner, or something else?
- Do you listen for an explicit statement of the gospel in a sermon? If not, what do you listen for? How do you know when you hear the gospel?

Chapter Four

How Do You Listen to Sermons?

While the group at St. Ambrose Church was discussing sermon models, Audrey noticed that Connie had become very quiet. "What are you thinking, Connie?" Audrey asked. "Well," Connie began slowly, "for a while, I've been thinking about joining a different church." The room fell silent as all eyes turned to Connie; everyone in the group looked stunned. Connie continued carefully. "Here at St. Ambrose, I've learned so much about who God is and what God expects of us. But, for a while now, that hasn't been enough for me. I need more than to know about God. I need to feel something. These conversations about preaching helped me realize that I don't listen to sermons with my mind; I listen to sermons with my emotions. My faith doesn't live in my head; my faith lives in my heart. Maybe I need to go to a church where preaching is more emotional, where I can feel something."

"I don't understand what you mean," Drew responded. "Most of us listen to sermons with our ears."

"Yes," Eleanor chimed in, "most of us *hear* sermons with our ears. Some people also take in sermons with their eyes; they watch Pastor Mark very intently. Other people sit with their eyes closed, and the kids in my Sunday school class look everywhere except at Pastor Mark, but they can still tell me what the sermon was about. As for me, I listen to sermons as if I am hearing them with my mother; I imagine I am talking the sermon over with her the way we used to before she died. I guess I listen to sermons through my relationship with my mother."

The notion that people listen to speeches, sermons, and other forms of communication differently is not new. Advertisers know that some people's perceptions of the messenger and the feelings the message creates are as important as the message itself. In chapter 3 you and I considered *what* people expect from sermons. In this chapter we explore *why* people might expect what they do from sermons. People's expectations of preaching are influenced by many factors, including their age, gender, learning style, cultural background, and social location. In this chapter, I consider how the nature of people's faith influences what they expect from preaching by asking, "How do you listen to sermons?" By discovering how we listen to sermons, we discover where our faith makes its home; we explore what our faith is like. We can better name what we hunger for, what we cling to, what we need to maintain a sense of control, and what we want and need the church to be. We learn how we practice and share our faith, and how we don't. Naming how we listen to sermons and considering where our faith makes its home help us discover the ways we connect the Christian faith and our lives.

What do you use to listen to sermons? Do you think sermons through in your head, feel sermons deeply in your heart, or use sermons to inform your actions? Perhaps you listen to sermons through your experience of holy places, such as the beauty of creation, or with the congregation as it worships. Maybe you listen to sermons because of, and in relation to, someone you consider a Christian mentor, an example, or a guide. Or perhaps you listen to sermons in the context of God and humanity's journey toward the world God intends. In this chapter, I identify eight ways people listen to sermons; seven places where our faith might make its home: (1) *head*, (2) *heart*, (3) *actions*, (4) *holy places*, (5) *worship*, (6) *mentoring*, and (7) *God's activity in the world*; and a final way people listen, (8) through faith that is *homeless*. Naming one of these, or somewhere else, as the place where our faith makes its home does not imply that our faith is lacking or absent in other areas of our lives; ideally, our Christian faith permeates all we are and everything we do. God desires that our faith is holistic and that we do not relegate our faith to one area of our lives, as surely as we ought not relegate our Christian faith to one day of the week. Yet, each of us has a place where our faith is most alive, most active, and most vivid. The faith that flows from that place

Figure 4.1. Where Faith Makes Its Home

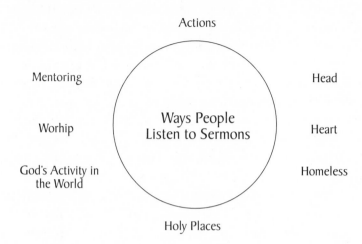

Actions

Mentoring

Head

Ways People
Listen to Sermons

Worhip

Heart

God's Activity in
the World

Homeless

Holy Places

enlivens all the other areas of our lives. In this chapter we tour
eight places where faith makes its home by considering how people
listen to sermons.

Head

Drew listens to sermons with his mind. Drew's faith makes its
home in his head. Listening to Connie talk about needing to feel
something, Drew feels a bit like Nicodemus listening to Jesus talk
about the reign of God. In John 3, Nicodemus works very hard
to think through and reason out what Jesus tells him about the
kingdom of God. Like the faith of Nicodemus, this kind of faith is
reasonable; seeks an orderly understanding of God's nature, creation, and our experience; and struggles with expressions of faith
that are not logical. For example, Nicodemus asks Jesus, "How
can anyone be born after having grown old? Can one enter a second time into the mother's womb and be born?" Jesus is not making sense to him. But Jesus also appeals to faith that is reasonable
when, in other Gospels, Jesus uses logic and reason to argue that

no one can serve two masters. Jesus is also very reasonable when he refutes the Pharisees and Sadducees.[1]

Drew and Christians whose faith makes its home in the head hold certain beliefs. For these Christians, the faithful are identified by the content of their beliefs and the degree of their conviction. Peter confesses the correct belief when he calls Jesus the Messiah but lacks conviction when Jesus defines *Messiah* in terms of his death on the cross. Then Peter rebukes him. Christians like Drew often conceptualize Christianity; this kind of faith is evident in the church's creeds, which were designed to answer abstract theological questions in a reasonable way and unite the church around its articulated faith. Faith that makes its home in the head connects to life by endeavoring to provide adequate answers to honest questions; this faith seeks ideas about how Christianity and life intersect in a given situation. In terms of evangelism, this faith recognizes that "belief becomes rationally expressed the moment it is shared with another person."[2] Christians therefore need the church to furnish words, statements, and content they can share.

People who listen to sermons with their mind desire preaching that provides information and ideas, which help them understand the significance of Scripture and the gospel for their lives. They seek answers to honest questions and appreciate sermons that are logical in both form and content. Preachers whose faith makes its home in the head tend to explain, persuade, and enforce the tenets of the faith. For example, these preachers believe that it is essential for Christians to understand the difference between resurrection and reincarnation, and assent to resurrection. For both preachers and hearers whose faith makes its home in the head, Scripture, as God's Word, provides the content of faith; that faith is best expressed systematically in doctrines, such as incarnation, justification, sanctification, sin, and grace.

For Drew, the sermon is the main event of the worship service. If worship did not include a sermon, Drew would probably not come to church. Drew desires the other parts of worship—hymns, prayers, choir anthems—to prepare for and support the sermon in ways that "make sense." Drew is most comfortable when the style of worship is cognitive and logical, often filled with words and lacking mystery and movement. Ritual acts, such as sacraments, need to be defined and explained. Music should be selected for its ability to correctly communicate the faith. Prayer must be thoughtful, well considered, and carefully crafted.

When faith that lives in the mind dominates, the congregation tends to be a community of people who hold certain beliefs in common. People may find themselves outside the church if they are unable or unwilling to assent to what the church teaches. The preacher is the authority, so leadership is hierarchical. The church's mission is to teach, persuade, convince, and correct so that the world knows the truth of the gospel.

Heart

Connie describes her faith as making its home in her heart. Connie yearns to feel rather than understand the gospel and to respond to God's love for her in genuine love for God, self, neighbor, and world. Connie identifies with the woman who anointed Jesus in the house of Simon the leper, particularly as Luke describes her— bathing Jesus's feet with her tears and drying them with her hair, kissing Jesus's feet and anointing them with costly ointment. Connie sees Jesus expressing faith that comes from his heart when he prays, "Father, forgive them; for they do not know what they are doing."[3]

For people like Connie, feeling is a way of knowing. Some people call it intuition, others the urging of the Spirit. The knowledge that comes through emotion can be so powerful that it affects people's values and actions; rather than responding rationally, people act according to their gut. Ronald J. Allen observes that, though individuals and groups frequently adopt ideas and pursue particular courses of action, in part because of their feelings, those powerful emotions may never rise to the level of consciousness. In fact, over time, people's feelings about ideas and behaviors may change without their ever being aware of it.[4]

Trust and mistrust are at the center of faith that expresses itself in and through emotion. For Connie, faith is trusting the gospel's assurance that God loves us and is active and involved in our lives. Christians like Connie are known by the depth or intensity of their trust in God and how that trust provides calm under stress. Jesus speaks to this kind of faith when he says things like, "Do not worry about your life, what you will eat or what you will drink, or about your body, what you will wear."[5] People whose faith lives in their heart do everything they can to solve a problem and then trust that God will do whatever else is needed. These people trust that God understands their situation and that God has the power and goodwill to bring good out of evil, even when they do not understand what that means or how that will happen.

Connie responds to preaching according to the feelings sermons rouse in her; she appreciates sermons that stir emotions she associates with divine presence, such as awe, closeness to God, and even judgment. Connie also values sermons that create emotions that reinforce the message of the sermon. "Don't just tell me to love my neighbor," Connie says. "Help me feel love for my neighbor." Stories are particularly effective for listeners like Connie. Connie also appreciates it when Scripture is presented and interpreted to evoke feelings, rather than explained. For example, rather than explicating the theological meaning and significance of Jesus's crucifixion, the preacher might help the congregation experience the depth of God's love in the severity of Jesus's suffering.

At times, what Connie feels during the sermon has nothing to do with the content of the sermon or the Scripture on which the sermon is based. Connie sometimes experiences feelings about God because of something in the worship service, what is happening in her life and in the life of the congregation, and even events occurring in the community and the world.

Connie has difficulty expressing her faith using words; she is intolerant of human-centered doctrines and secretly resents the church for insisting upon them. Connie has no patience for theological differences that keep Christians apart. Yet, Connie appreciates sermons that put her feelings about God into words, because they help her better respond to what she is feeling. As she said, Connie desires preaching and worship to evoke feelings in those gathered; for Connie, the goal of worship and preaching is to inspire rather than to inform and instruct. As Connie sees it, worship should produce feelings, because high commitment and deep trust are more likely to develop in an emotionally charged atmosphere.

We retain what we feel, particularly what we celebrate. Music, movement, and spontaneous participation are important elements of the service. Prayer is less formal, may even be formless, and is distinguished by its sense of holy desire. Feeling in worship is often regarded as an indication of the presence and work of the Holy Spirit, verifying the truth and trustworthiness of the message of the sermon. Feeling in worship also connects people to one another, creating a sense of community and even a corporate identity. For this to happen, worship needs to be a safe place to experience and express emotion, and worship leaders must not intentionally manipulate people's feelings. Whether in worship or in the world, the church's mission is to help people feel God's love and have a close relationship with Christ by sharing that love in the world.

Actions

Audrey's faith makes its home in her actions. Audrey resonates with James's assertion that faith without works is dead[6] and loves to quote St. Francis, who said, "Preach the Gospel always. . . . If necessary, use words." Audrey takes Jesus's description of the last judgment most seriously. Jesus identifies those blessed by his Father in terms of their actions. Jesus names the faithful as those who feed the hungry, clothe the naked, care for the sick, welcome the stranger, visit those in prison and, without looking for a reward and even realizing what they are doing, do for Christ as they do for the least of these.[7] People like Audrey, whose faith makes its home in their actions, seek a way of life that pleases God. Some are concerned with obeying God's commands in order to minimize pain and ensure God's blessing. Others desire to live lives congruent with the life of Christ by taking up their cross and sharing in Christ's suffering for the sake of the world.

Audrey looks for direction from God through the sermon. She desires preaching that tells her what God expects of people individually and as a congregation. Some whose faith makes its home in their actions listen to sermons to learn the rules they are to live by. The Ten Commandments and instructions like those Jesus seems to give in the Sermon on the Mount are important to them. Preachers often present Jesus as the ultimate example or role model and exhort parishioners to be like him. Other people whose faith makes its home in their actions, including Audrey, prefer sermons that equip them to determine God's will and purpose in their life by providing a framework for Christian living, rather than absolute prescriptions. Audrey remembers a particularly helpful sermon in which Pastor Mark considered what it means to "love your neighbor as yourself" without telling the congregation what to do. Now, as she seeks to live faithfully, Audrey asks herself, "What is the loving thing to do?" Whether they seek concrete moral imperatives to live by or a framework for determining how to live faithfully, people whose faith lives in their actions look for God's will and direction in the Bible and in preaching.

Worship forms and empowers people to live as God's people. People's piety often centers on protocol, approaching God properly by doing things right in worship and behaving appropriately, particularly in church. Spontaneity makes people like Audrey uncomfortable. Forgiveness and the opportunity to begin again are often emphasized in worship. Making confession and receiving absolution are an especially important part of the service. People understand Holy Communion as God's forgiveness and that they are to prepare themselves by examining their conscience so that they receive Communion worthily. Receiving the Lord's Supper too frequently diminishes the gift. Movement such as kneeling to pray may be a meaningful part of worship. Prayers often ask God to help the congregation and its members to do something, rather than asking God to do it directly. Both the lyrics and tone of music used in worship are often very serious.

For those whose faith makes its home in their actions, the congregation is a community committed to a certain lifestyle, which they often perceive as very different from the way people live in the world. Congregation members support one another in their Christian life. The preacher, on behalf of the community, exemplifies, directs, enforces, judges, corrects, and forgives those committed to the Christian way of life. The church's mission is to do all it can to resist the sinful world and promote the way of life that God desires and prescribes.

Holy Places

Gail said that she decided not to participate in the conversations about preaching because, most Sundays, Gail has no idea what the sermon is about and doesn't really care. Gail does not come to church to listen to the sermon or even to participate in the service. Gail comes to church to be in church—to come into God's presence, to be still before her maker, to quiet her spirit, to ground and center her life. For Gail, the church is a building where God lives. It's the tabernacle, the holy of holies. The cross, lighted candles, beautiful stained-glass windows, and ministers opening the Bible and praying at the altar are all signs that God is present in this holy place.

For Christians like Gail, faith makes its home in holy places, such as the beauty of a sunset over the water, the quiet rooms of a hospice, and the sacredness of a worship space. Some people are most keenly aware of God's presence and purpose for us and all life when they are in these kinds of places, and so they return to them again and again. The Gospel writers tell us that Jesus withdrew to mountains by himself to pray and made his way to Gethsemane at the Mount of Olives to pray, as was his custom, on the night before he died. People may also regard specific places as holy because that is where they experienced profound or intense encounters with God. The Gospel of Mark might chide Peter for wanting to build three dwellings at the site of Jesus's transfiguration; however, the Hebrew Scriptures are filled with accounts of biblical characters, including Abraham, Jacob, Moses, Samson, and Samuel, who name places for encounters with the Holy that occurred there. For centuries Christian pilgrims have made their way to the Holy Land in order to encounter Christ in the places of his life and ministry.

For people whose faith makes its home in holy places, the church is first and foremost a place where they go to encounter God. These Christians are particularly aware that they are coming into God's presence, standing on holy ground, when they enter the worship space. They act reverently and expect others to do the same. This understanding of faith helps to explain why some congregations seem more committed to their building than to the congregation's ministry. The memories and history of God's profound encounters, both in people's own lives and in the lives of beloved brothers and sisters in Christ who have gone before them, are contained in its walls. Furnishings like pews, altar, baptismal font, and pulpit are tangible touchstones to those experiences.

For some like Gail whose faith makes its home in holy places, what happens in the sermon is less important than that the sermon happens. Preaching is itself a place of God's presence. This kind of faith takes seriously that some people, and all people at some time, need God's presence as well as (and perhaps more than) good news. Yet, in addition to being locations of encounters with God, preaching and worship can facilitate such encounters, particularly as an experience of dying and rising; preaching and worship tangibly address both our need of and dependence upon God and the gift of God's presence, grace, and power. These encounters are both actual and vicarious. The worship space, the music, the fellowship of the congregation, a part of the liturgy, something in a sermon, and the sacraments might all provide actual encounters with God. Scripture, testimony, and stories told in sermons might provide vicarious encounters with God, as people enter into fellowship with biblical, historical, or contemporary characters and their encounters with God. Scripture, sermon, story, and testimony also provide a guide to how we experience God in other places. For example, Scripture invites us to expect God's presence in the midst of suffering and to listen for God to speak in a still, small voice. Both actual and visceral encounters with God are real and meaningful.

This kind of faith does not insist that God is present in some places and absent in others. After all, God creates and blesses everything. God's blessing makes all creation the sign and means of God's presence, wisdom, love, and revelation. God blesses the world, blesses humanity, blesses time. God fills all that exists with God's love and goodness so that we know God and live in relationship with God. Certain locations—where God's presence and purpose are more readily accessible—point to, hint at, and help us apprehend and trust God's presence and purpose in places where we experience God as distant or absent. Outside the church, Christians with this kind of faith may be identified by their awareness of God's presence; some with this kind of faith describe themselves as "spiritual" rather than "religious." Inside the church, Christians often measure this kind of faith by people's connection to the church as the place of an encounter with God, such as the manifestation of a spiritual gift, an identifiable experience of salvation, or participation in a rite such as Confirmation. Through such encounters and by returning to places in which they experience God's presence, people's faith and hope are renewed and they feel motivated to love. This faith is contagious.

Worship

Pastor Mark thought out loud, "For me it's not the worship space; it's the congregation as it worships. I prepare and listen to sermons through the congregation as it worships." When members of the congregation pray and sing, say the creed, offer their gifts, and celebrate the sacraments, Pastor Mark hears the people of God proclaim the gospel. Pastor Mark reflected, "When the congregation preaches well, I experience my preaching to be more empowered because my spirit is uplifted. When I can listen to Scripture read well by a member of the congregation, the texts from which I will preach become the living family stories of this people of faith. When the congregation really sings hymns prior to the sermon, I feel enfolded in prayer." Pastor Mark mused that the shepherds proclaimed Christ's birth in response to the angels' song. He continues, "I am particularly partial to the congregation singing psalms. I like to close my eyes and listen and hear the congregation pray using words God's people have offered up for generations. I go to the pulpit cloaked in their prayer." Pastor Mark admits that, immediately after he says the amen that concludes the sermon, he is eager to know whether the message was heard and received. He can tell by the way the congregation sings the sermon hymn and prays. He also says that he takes comfort that, when a sermon doesn't go well, the choir and minister of music usually proclaim God's grace and make up for it.

For people like Pastor Mark, and they are not all pastors, faith is nourished by and expresses itself through the congregation as it worships. More than something they feel or experience, these Christians regard the church's worship as God's way of gathering, forming, and sending the church into the world. In worship God uses the entire congregation to proclaim the gospel. Worship is often characterized by mystery, silence, and movement. Music is an especially powerful way that God speaks and the congregation responds. Prayer is corporate in nature, structured so that everyone can participate, and offered in the hope that all will add their amen. Anything in the service—a hymn, a prayer, the sermon, or an old couple holding each other up on their way to Communion—may be the way God proclaims good news that day. Whatever the style, people whose faith makes its home in the church's worship insist that worship be allowed to speak for itself or, better, that the congregation trust God to speak and act in and through worship. They resent leaders that provide ongoing commentary, set the mood, or give stage directions. This faith is often measured in terms of how people participate in, understand, and value Christian worship.

Those whose faith makes its home in worship believe that Scripture as God's Word is meant to be proclaimed publicly and interpreted communally, rather than read privately and interpreted individually. They trust God to speak through the words of prophets and apostles and that the church hears the voice of Christ when Scripture is read and heard in worship. Scripture unites the congregation as the community gathers around God's Word; Scripture also unites the church across time and throughout the world as, on any given Sunday, the same passages are often read and heard. Scripture read and heard in worship also determines the proclamation of faith as the church selects from the Bible those passages it deems significant and gives them prominence in worship. These are passages that have given the church insight in the past and to which the church returns again and again. Readings are removed from the books in which they are found and placed in the context of the Sunday on which they are read, the worship life of the church, and the people of God at prayer. While preachers need to know the historical and literary context of a passage in order to remain faithful to the biblical witness, preachers also need to decide what and how much of the passage's historical and literary context the congregation needs to be told in a sermon and why.

The sermon is an essential part of worship. These Christians appreciate preaching that relates to the rest of the service and that communicates the gospel in a way that motivates and empowers the congregation to respond by giving God thanks and praise in worship. When the sermon and other elements of the service, such as hymns and prayers, are coordinated, the congregation's worship reinforces the message of the sermon and provides the congregation with the words, actions, and opportunity to respond to that message in faith. These folk are less concerned about whether the preacher had a good sermon than they are that the congregation had meaningful worship.

The church is a worshiping community. Worship is the most important thing a congregation does, from which everything else follows. These Christians embrace a description of the apostolic church provided in Acts: "Those who welcomed [the] message were baptized. . . . They devoted themselves to the apostles' teaching and fellowship, to the breaking of bread and the prayers."[8] The entire congregation is responsible for worship. Clergy do not worship for or on behalf of the people. While the pastor is called to exercise certain gifts within the congregation's worship, every other member of the congregation is also called to use his or her gifts for this purpose.

For these Christians, the church's mission is to worship. Christians worshiping offer a powerful witness to their faith, common life, and the life and purpose to which God calls all creation. Still, people may feel excluded by their unfamiliarity with the service. Recognizing that becoming part of any community takes time as people learn its ways, congregations do not express hospitality by reinventing their worship. Rather, they allow visitors to spend time on the edge of the congregation, answering their questions about the service and helping them participate. The church trusts that, through worship, God will teach and form visitors in faith, as surely as God equips God's people to live as Christ's body in the world. In this regard, the church worships for the sake of the world.

Mentoring

Eleanor listens to sermons as if she is hearing them with her mother. All her life, Eleanor looked to her mother as a Christian mentor, someone who modeled for Eleanor aspects of the journey that is growing in the life of faith. By following her mother's journey through an issue or experience, Eleanor learned how to faithfully journey through her own issues and experiences. Eleanor especially valued listening to and discussing sermons with her mother. Now that her mother is gone, Eleanor continues to process sermons by imagining what her mother would think and say. Eleanor's faith makes its home in her relationship with this Christian mentor.

For people whose faith makes its home in this kind of relationship, their Christian mentor does not need to be someone with whom they have a close relationship. Their mentor may be someone that they only know about, such as a famous church leader, an author, or someone from Christian history. Some might consider a respected member of the congregation or the pastor as mentors. Regardless of who their mentor is, people whose faith makes its home in such a relationship give authority to someone they respect and trust, and listen to sermons in dialogue with that person. Paul explicitly offers himself to the Thessalonians as a mentor. Timothy's mother and grandmother were his Christian mentors.[9] The church remembers and celebrates saints as mentors.

For some Christians, the preacher serves as a Christian mentor. This relationship might develop through personal interaction, as the pastor lovingly and effectively responds to people's spiritual needs. Alternatively, parishioners may only know the pastor through Sunday worship, where the pastor's quality preaching provides wisdom and insight and the pastor's worship leadership fosters unity and stability in a complicated world. When the preacher is the Christian mentor, the sermon functions as testimony. The preacher's reflections on her or his experience serve as the lens through which listeners can consider and reflect upon their own experience and encounter the gospel. When statements and lifestyle conform to each other, the preacher's life is evidence that the congregation can trust the content of the message. This congruence, combined with presence emanating from the preacher, leads listeners to experience resonance between the preacher, the message, and themselves. When the preacher is not the mentor, listeners participate in, evaluate, and respond to sermons by filtering them through what they have learned from their mentor, as well as the mentor's own evaluation and response, be that actual or extrapolated. This relationship influences the way these listeners respond to the form and delivery of sermons, as well as their content.

As the author of Hebrews indicates, Scripture is the treasury of the lives of God's faithful people, who are themselves mentors for us. Their journeys of faith inform and guide us so that, "since we are surrounded by so great a cloud of witnesses, [we can] also lay aside every weight and the sin that clings so closely, and . . . run with perseverance the race that is set before us."[10] Scripture provides examples of lives of faith that we can imitate and emulate as we seek to live faithfully. Listeners interpret Scripture themselves and consider and evaluate others' interpretations of Scripture, including the preacher's, according to their mentors, whether they are biblical, historical, confessional, or contemporary.

For these Christians, worship is, as Barbara Brown Taylor suggests, a Christian family album. Taylor writes, "Our liturgy bears the marks of those who've gone before us—portraits of those we have never met, inscriptions written in many different hands, bits and pieces of treasured correspondence, favorite recipes, prayers, and remedies—all of them left for us by our ancestors in the faith, who have bequeathed us their manual for approaching God."[11] These Christians appreciate worship as they have "always" done it. They may be slow to embrace change, in part, because change signals a break with those who have gone before them. As I said previously, the order of worship, favorite hymns, the church building, and worship furnishings are touchstones to mentors, whose presence can still be felt, even though they are no longer there.

For these Christians, the church is the communion of saints. The congregation is part of something greater than itself, the body of Christ of all times and in all places. While these Christians may feel especially close to the saints who have gone before them in that place, they are also aware of and strengthened by their connection to Christians throughout history and around the world. This connection finds tangible expression in lectionary and creed, as well as the congregation's cooperation with other churches locally, a commitment to benevolence, and an awareness of and participation in shared mission globally. Passing on the faith to children and nurturing future leaders for the congregation are primary concerns within the congregation. These Christians express and share their faith by humbly seeking to follow in their mentors' footsteps and live exemplary Christian lives.

God's Activity in the World

Fred is more concerned about what is happening in the world than what is happening in church. In fact, Fred sees no point to anything that happens in church that is not relevant to God's intent for and activity in the world. "Since God so loved *the world* that God gave the only Son," Fred says, "I cannot imagine a personal relationship with Jesus Christ that is not inextricably linked to love for neighbor and all creation." Christians like Fred, whose faith makes its home in God's will for and activity in the world, regard Jesus's inaugural sermon at the synagogue in Nazareth, as it is recorded by Luke, as the heart of Jesus's mission, and a social rather than a spiritual proclamation.[12] For these Christians, salvation that is defined as "going to heaven" is part of and even subordinate to Jesus's work of righting this world and restoring the cosmos to God. For these Christians, all things in heaven and on earth were created in Christ. Christ holds all things together. In Christ God reconciles all things.[13] Faith that makes its home in God's activity in the world is measured in terms of openness to the new thing that God is doing. These Christians are attuned to God's intention, activity, and nearness in the world and to the powers, structures, and systems that are contrary and opposed to God.

As part of God's activity in the world, the church is a "community of friends."[14] In this community, friends of Jesus love one another and the world, as Jesus loved them—giving their lives for each other and for the world. Together, the community discerns and proclaims God's intent for and activity in the world, names and points to both the signs of the nearness of God's reign and the forces opposed to God that are at work in the world, and embodies life in God's reign through practices that help them live out the gospel perspective in concrete circumstances. Through these practices, the church resists the powers of death at work in the world and lives a concrete alternative to the world as it is. For example, by practicing stewardship, giving things away rather than keeping them, the church resists greed and selfishness and embodies God's intention that all have enough. As a community of friends, the congregation shares responsibility for discerning and embodying God's will and ways in the world.

As God's Word, Scripture provides the core beliefs that define the Christian community. The narratives of God's interaction with humanity and creation contained in the Bible disclose God's will and activity in the world. Scripture may provide a vision of the world as God intends, as Jesus does in the Beatitudes, particularly in Luke's Gospel. Scripture might challenge both the world as it is and the church's participation in it. Scripture might make claims about how the righteous are to respond to systemic injustice. Scripture certainly provides a perspective with which the church evaluates itself, as well as human and global situations. Regardless of how a biblical passage and the world interpret one another, the church looks to Scripture to discern God's intent for and way of being in the world. Telling and retelling these stories forms the community's identity and shapes how Christians and congregations understand and live in the world.

Preaching and worship are practices indispensable to the church's mission of proclaiming the in-breaking of God's reign, resisting the deadly ways of forces opposed to God, and embodying the world that God intends. Worship provides Christians with an orientation toward the world, helping Christians to see the world as God sees it and as God intends it. In worship and preaching, the church tells and retells its stories, interpreting them for the contemporary world and enacting the interactions with God recorded in Scripture, which define the church's identity. In worship, the church also praises God for the gift of love in Jesus Christ and is formed and empowered to share in Christ's life by giving itself in love for the sake of the world. Worship is itself an act of resistance because, when we worship God in Christ, we cannot worship forces opposed to God, such as self-sufficiency, instant gratification, material possession, and power over others, which covet our adoration and loyalty.

Preaching is also essential to the church's identity and mission. As I said in chapter 1, Jesus chose preaching to oppose violent domination and make known the reign of God. Like the preaching of Jesus, the church's preaching does not silently and passively accept systems and structures that are contrary to God. Nor does the church's preaching participate in domination by coercing belief or forcing an agenda. Instead, the church's preaching, like the preaching of Jesus, gives people the freedom to decide, choose, and express their faith. Preaching accomplishes this by naming the forces opposed to God; exposing their deadly ways, which often seem like common sense; and offering a vision of God's new creation. Drawing on Scripture, the preacher proposes both a vision of God's activity in the world and practices that flow from and are a way to participate in that vision. By doing this in ways that are neither dominating nor coercive, preaching provides the basis for and facilitates the congregation's ongoing discernment and dialogue. Regardless of what happens in that conversation, preaching is an essential way the church resists the forces opposed to God by offering an alternative reality and way of being in a manner that affords people the freedom and dignity that God intends for all creation.

Homeless

Brian stared at the graphic of ways people listen to sermons. "I listen to sermons with my eyes, as if I am searching for something," Brian said. "I guess my faith is 'homeless.'" Brian's faith is very real; however, rather than being settled, it is restless. At times, Brian's faith searches, questions, challenges. At other times, it is indifferent and content. Brian's faith is both skeptical and curious, cynical and hope filled. Brian recalls that Jesus said, "Foxes have holes, and birds of the air have nests; but the Son of Man has nowhere to lay his head."[15] Brian muses that his faith has nowhere to lay its head; it is homeless.

Brian is very interested in God; Brian is less interested in church, which he often finds boring, irrelevant, and hypocritical. For people like Brian, whose faith is homeless, the church is a foreign culture, sometimes an unsafe place. They wish the church would judge others less and talk with others more. They get frustrated when congregations get caught up in preserving the status quo, surviving, pleasing members, and saving money, rather than proclaiming the gospel and meeting the needs of the community.

People like Brian whose faith is homeless desire worship that is upbeat, well done, related to Scripture, visitor sensitive, and relevant. They desire an atmosphere in church that is warm and friendly, where they feel welcome and accepted, and worship that is informal. These folk want a personal experience with God. In terms of the worship service itself, people whose faith is homeless want to understand the Savior before they understand the service. People with this kind of faith prefer an entire worship service, including the sermon, built around a theme that is important to the community. They appreciate music that is contemporary and personal. Worship that appeals to people whose faith is homeless is heavy on presentation; singing one chorus during a service is about all the participation they can muster. Because the church is an unfamiliar culture, traditional symbols, such as ministers wearing robes and even the cross, are removed from the worship space. Some congregations even change the location of worship, taking the service outside, to a fellowship hall, or somewhere in the community, like a coffee shop.

People whose faith is homeless desire preaching that is positive. They want upbeat, relevant sermons. They do not want to hear how bad or wrong people and things are. Rather, they want to know where they can find hope, joy, love, and peace. These folk want to hear about the intimacy of God. They want preaching that is practical. More important than hearing how to get to heaven, they want to hear how God helps them get through the week. Because Scripture is unfamiliar and religious language is foreign, these people appreciate sermons that express the gospel in the language of the culture. They also appreciate thematic or topical preaching that brings Scripture to bear on their concerns. Sermon series are especially helpful.

Evangelism is the top priority of congregations that seek to minister to people whose faith is homeless; the church's mission is to make disciples. Jesus's parables of the lost sheep and the lost coin and his ministry to people on the fringes provide compelling biblical models for these congregations. The business of Sunday morning is to welcome visitors and meet people's needs. Evangelism is not understood as a "special gift" or "the pastor's job." Everyone is involved in evangelism. While worship introduces people to Jesus, small group ministry provides the entry point to the congregation, as ministry occurs person to person. Loving and visiting individuals is the responsibility of the congregation, rather than the pastor. The pastor relates to groups in order to provide the vision for mission and keep the congregation on course.

Now that you and I have considered where our faith makes its home, we can explore how sermons intersect with our faith in ways that impact our daily lives. This is the subject of chapter 5.

Questions for Discussion

- Are you a member of your congregation because of what it teaches, the way members live, or the way you feel when you are there? Do you think your pastor would be a member of this church if she or he was not the pastor? Why or why not?
- Where does your faith make its home? Or do you find that your faith moves around from place to place?
- Do you express your faith best in words, actions, your personal relationship with Christ, or some other way?
- How are you most keenly aware of God's presence?
- Who is one of your Christian mentors?
- How could someone whose faith is homeless inform your congregation's preaching?
- What one question would you like to ask someone whose faith is homeless? How do the other locations inform preaching? What questions would you ask people with these kinds of faith?

Chapter Five

How Do You Connect Sermons and Daily Life?

Eleanor was beside herself. In her almost 80 years, Eleanor could not recall ever feeling as angry, stunned, and disappointed as she was by what her church had done. Or, rather, by what the people of St. Ambrose Church refused to do. Rev. John Parson, pastor of a neighboring congregation, had served his flock and the entire community faithfully and well for many years. Rev. Parson was loved and respected by everyone. So, when rumors of a relationship with another man began to circulate, and those rumors turned into accusations that resulted in Rev. Parson's resignation from his church, "for the sake of the ministry," his congregation was fractured and the community in shock. The scandal seemed to reach into every congregation in town, and so the local council of churches called a meeting to figure out how to respond. Each congregation was invited to send the pastor and a member, so Eleanor went with Pastor Mark.

The people at the meeting had many different opinions about what Rev. Parson had or had not done. But, after several hours of conversation that went from polite to heated to prayerful, everyone agreed that, regardless of what had happened, Rev. Parson's wife and children had done nothing wrong and that Rev. Parson's resignation from his church put the family in a real financial mess. Recalling Paul's words to the Corinthians, "If one member suffers, all suffer together with it" (1 Cor. 12:26), and knowing firsthand that these words are true, the council of churches made a financial gift to the Parson family, authorized a collection on the family's behalf, and asked each congregation to contribute. Eleanor left the meeting convinced of the Spirit's leading and that the religious community was making an unexpected and a powerful witness.

The people of St. Ambrose Church held a congregational meeting the next Sunday to vote to make a gift to the collection. Once
again, it seemed to Eleanor that the Spirit was at work, because
the Gospel text appointed in the lectionary for that Sunday was
Matthew 18:21-35, the parable of the unforgiving servant. Pastor
Mark preached poignantly about all our sin and powerfully about
God's forgiveness in Christ. Then, with unusual force and clarity,
Pastor Mark preached that we are the forgiven servants presented
with an opportunity to extend God's forgiveness to another in a
tangible way. But at the congregational meeting that followed the
service, it did not seem to Eleanor that people heard the sermon.
They talked about "getting what you deserve." They said they
could not comprehend how the council could ask them to sacrifice
part of their treasury for someone who "made his own bed and
now had to lie in it." Eleanor was most upset because friends, who
often criticized Pastor Mark for not preaching clearly about what
it means to live a Christian life, were appalled that he would dare
to tell the congregation what to do with its money. It seemed to
Eleanor that her friends wanted Pastor Mark to tell other people
how they ought to live but not members of the congregation. In
the end, the people of St. Ambrose Church decided that, while
individuals could certainly donate to the collection for the Parson
family, they would give nothing as a congregation. At the next
meeting of the preaching group, Eleanor asked, "What's the point
of preaching if people don't connect sermons to their real lives?"

I previously asserted that the Sunday sermon is the most prominent way the church brings the resources of the Christian faith to
bear on the daily lives of the vast majority of practicing Christians,
and that both preachers and people who listen to sermons desire
and expect preaching to connect with daily life. I reported that
Christians are excited to discuss sermons that connect the Christian faith and contemporary life and lament sermons that unplug
Christianity from real life. So why did Pastor Mark's sermon fail
to produce the desired result? In chapter 1, I proposed several possible reasons why things like this happen. The sermon may not
have been able to overcome competing external messages and internal values, and so the result proposed by the council of churches
and Pastor Mark required people to move too far too fast. Jesus's

own sermon at the synagogue in Nazareth failed precisely because, though Jesus announced the year of the Lord's favor and all that meant for those afflicted and oppressed, Jesus did not announce God's vindication upon sinners and oppressors. Like the people in Nazareth, perhaps the people of St. Ambrose were not convinced that this was the complete—and, therefore, authentic—word from the Lord. Perhaps the people of St. Ambrose were not looking for sermons that connect the Christian faith and their daily lives by directing them to respond to a situation in a specific manner.

How do you connect the sermon to your daily life? Considering what we expect to happen in preaching is akin to considering how we expect God to answer prayer. Do we expect God to do something, to direct and help us do something, to be present with us, or to help us accept things as they are? Do we pray because we expect an immediate answer to every prayer or because, over time, we have found praying to be beneficial? What about preaching? Do we measure preaching by the immediate impact or result of an individual sermon or the long-term effect of preaching over time? While our consumer culture and need for instant gratification might lead us to demand immediate results and to insist that every sermon give everyone in worship something directly related to their individual lives, the adaptive work, which I discussed in chapter 1, for which preaching is best suited takes time. For example, to create positive images of those people congregants consider "other," preaching proceeds slowly, week after week, year after year. By deliberately attending to multiple perspectives and speaking to the complexity of issues, this slow process changes minds, softens hearts, and instills motivation.

So how do you hope preaching will influence your daily life? As is the case with prayer, our answer may vary day to day and week to week, depending on what is happening in our individual or communal life. The way we connect preaching and life will certainly be informed by and reflect how we understand the gospel, and in what ways and to what extent we allow the gospel to govern and work in our individual and communal lives. How we expect preaching to affect our lives also influences the way we understand Christian community and Christian mission. If, for example, we expect every sermon to directly relate to the individual lives of

Figure 5.1. How Do You Connect Preaching and Life?

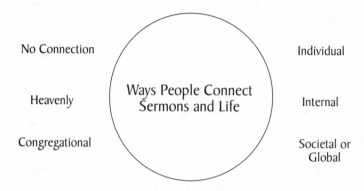

everyone in worship, the congregation will need to be homogeneous and the congregation's mission needs to attract people who fit the profile.

In this chapter, I propose six ways that people, both those who listen and those who preach, relate sermons to their daily lives. Some make (1) *no connection* between preaching and real life. Others make a (2) *heavenly*, (3) *internal*, (4) *individual*, (5) *congregational*, or (6) *societal or global* connection. Equally important, some people, both preachers and congregants, consider some of these ways of connecting preaching and daily life inappropriate, particularly if the preacher makes the connection explicit in the sermon. For example, while some congregations invite political candidates into their pulpits to assess the candidates' faith and how they relate it to their politics, other congregations would be scandalized if the preacher explicitly addressed a social issue from the pulpit and even mentioned a candidate by name. More common is when members of a congregation and their preacher differ in how they relate the gospel to daily life and the sermon may not connect. Therefore, people may leave worship feeling disappointed.

No Connection

"What's the point of preaching if people don't connect sermons to their real lives?" Eleanor's question hung in the air.

"Then I've heard a lot of pointless preaching," Brian finally responded, "sermons that don't even try to connect with real life. Why do you suppose anyone would preach like that?"

"Some of my colleagues say that witnessing people's lack of response to sermons has convinced them that preaching is pointless," Pastor Mark answered. "They've decided that people don't listen and that nothing will ever change. They're so disillusioned that they've all but stopped preaching. They figure that, since preaching doesn't matter, they can throw a sermon together Saturday night or even Sunday morning, and spend their time and energy on ministries that, to them, really make a difference."

"Yes," Audrey countered, "and some preachers are so concerned about being practical and relevant that the Bible, and even the gospel, seems to get left out of the sermon."

Sermons that people perceive do not connect with real life result from one of three things—(1) poor preaching, (2) intentionally presenting the faith as unrelated to life, and (3) working too hard to be relevant. Stated simply, the first kind of sermon that does not connect with daily life results from poor preaching. Poor preaching can occur on account of the preacher, the congregation, or both. Preachers might lack the skill, time, or commitment to engage in careful and serious sermon preparation and delivery. Sermons that intersect and interact with contemporary life and interpret our everyday experience through the lens of Scripture and the gospel are hard to prepare. When preparation is lacking, the chances are good that the sermon will be as well. For their part, congregants may abandon any hope that the Christian message has anything to say to their lives and stop listening altogether. Or listeners may neglect to prepare themselves to listen to sermons or be so distracted or inattentive during the sermon that the message is lost on them. Finally, both preachers and parishioners might bring expectations to sermons that are impossible for even the best preaching to meet. When expectations are too high, when the preacher is not prepared, or when the congregation is not open to the possibility that the sermon will be a meaningful word from God, sermons rarely overcome such obstacles. When preacher and congregation do not expect the sermon to be a word from God and people, even so, experience a connection between the gospel and their lives, it is the work of the Holy Spirit.

I often describe the second type of sermon that does not connect to daily life as "teaching for the sake of knowledge." Some
people, listeners as well as preachers, do not want preaching to
connect with daily life. They worry that Christians do not know
the faith. They are particularly concerned that the faithful are
"biblically illiterate," that is, that Christians are unfamiliar with
even the basic stories and content of the Bible. These Christians
advocate preaching that is, in essence, teaching. Some want sermons to be Bible studies that explain what texts meant in the
ancient world in a way that helps people understand Scripture
better and generates such love for God's Word that people open
their Bibles. A sermon on Jesus's inaugural sermon might explain
the situation in Nazareth at the start of Jesus's ministry and how
he interprets the passage from Isaiah. Some preachers and hearers
also desire preaching that approaches Christian doctrine in this
same way. They think sermons ought to explain theology and
doctrine so that people correctly understand what the church believes and teaches. Those who appreciate this approach to preaching consider the Bible and the Christian message to be so important that they are not concerned when the sermon does not relate
the message to contemporary life. They do not worry about how
the sermon is received by the congregation, because they believe
God promises to be present when the Scriptures are faithfully
preached. They trust that when people learn the meaning of the
Bible and the doctrines of the faith, this knowledge will influence
their lives.

The third type of sermon that some find disconnected from
daily life downplays the Bible and an explicit Christian message,
instead presenting the relevance of God and the congregation
to people's everyday lives. Tom Long describes sermons that are
saturated with context and in need of a healthy dose of biblical
and theological content.[1] In these sermons, preachers begin with
a problem that is a serious concern to the listeners, rather than a
biblical text, and demonstrate how spiritual insights and congregational programs help people address it. These problems often include topics like parenting skills, time and financial management,
and relationship difficulties. If such a sermon were connected to
Luke's account of Jesus's inaugural sermon, it might center on the

ways congregation members feel impoverished, captive, and oppressed and how God and the congregation can help people address those feelings. This preaching is very practical in order to
meet people's need for instant gratification. According to Long,
while these sermons are full of religious language, calls for spiritual growth, and reassurances that God loves us, they often lack
a deep sense of the gospel as "news"; as something that God has
done, is doing, and will do that stands out from the routine events
of life and makes a potentially life-changing difference.[2] Instead,
the gospel functions as "a tool placed in the preacher's hands to be
used to fix whatever problems and solve whatever puzzles people
bring to church."[3] This preaching is so grounded in the congregation that, rather than proclaiming the cross and resurrection of
Christ, God is presented in a way that meets people's needs.

People who do not experience a connection between preaching and their lives have no choice but to compartmentalize the
"sacred" things of God and the "secular" things of the world.
They distinguish between the spiritual and the material, the faith
we hold on Sunday and the common sense we use to negotiate the rest of the week. For parishioners who hold this view,
preaching dwells on the periphery of their existence. Pastors who
see no connection between preaching and life sometimes become
convinced of the futility of preaching. They distinguish between
preaching and the church's *real* mission of evangelism, justice
making, or care and nurture. These pastors gravitate to roles
they deem more important; they become activists, evangelists,
congregational CEOs, counselors, or community leaders. Over
time, worship and preaching become secondary to the congregation, until the connection between worship and mission is
severed.

Heavenly

"What about sermons that tell us how to get to heaven?" Drew
asked. "Surely, that's what preaching is supposed to be about."
On some level, salvation, receiving or entering into eternal life, is
a concern that most preachers and churchgoers bring to the ser-

mon. For those who make a heavenly connection between preaching and their daily life, salvation is the chief concern of preaching. These preachers and hearers distinguish between this world and the world to come; they are primarily concerned with the life to come and how our life in this world will affect our participation in it. Some want to know how to get to heaven. Others need assurance that they are going to a better place. Still others seek assurance that God will welcome them into heaven.

"Then someone came to [Jesus] and said, 'Teacher, what good deed must I do to have eternal life?'" People who make a heavenly connection in preaching understand that, at one time or another, we are all that someone. Listeners are concerned with what they must do to have eternal life and preachers are concerned to tell them. The answer varies in Scripture. Jesus told that someone to keep the commandments, "sell your possessions, and give the money to the poor, and you will have treasure in heaven; then come, follow me."[4] Elsewhere in the New Testament, having eternal life is less about actions and more about attitude, specifically an attitude of belief. "For God so loved the world that he gave his only Son, so that everyone who believes in him may not perish but may have eternal life." In John, Jesus also declares, "This is indeed the will of my Father, that all who see the Son and believe in him may have eternal life; and I will raise them up on the last day."[5] Mark introduces a religious rite into the equation: "The one who believes and is baptized will be saved."[6] Drawing on Scripture, Billy Graham describes another ritual, telling people they can be born again and have new life by coming forward, repenting of their sin, and accepting Christ as their personal Lord and Savior. In Matthew and Mark, Jesus promises that those who endure hardship and persecution for the faith will be saved.[7] A sermon on Jesus's inaugural sermon might tell hearers that they are to bring good news to the poor and help the blind to see and the oppressed go free. Regardless of what answer preachers give, preaching that addresses the question of what one must do to receive eternal life makes a heavenly connection to daily life in its call for Christian discipleship, a way of life that resists the temptations of this world and is disciplined by faith.

To inspire the faithful to believe in Jesus, live as disciples of Christ, resist temptation, and endure suffering and even persecution for the gospel's sake, some sermons make a heavenly connection to ordinary life by distinguishing between this world and the world to come. "Then I saw a new heaven and a new earth; for the first heaven and the first earth had passed away."[8] These sermons then proclaim the world that is coming is better—a feast of rich food and well-aged wine for all people; a time when God will swallow up death, wipe away all tears, and remove all shame and disgrace from the earth.[9] Or, in the language of Jesus's inaugural sermon, God will bring a time when the poor receive good news, those who are blind see, captives are released, and the oppressed go free. Because the church is the harbinger of this new age, the church's preaching witnesses to God's coming reign. For many, the church serves as a beacon of hope and provides a haven or sanctuary from the hostile world. Preachers and listeners might therefore resist introducing topics and conversations that may not accomplish anything but will certainly disturb the peace.[10] Instead, by focusing on the coming reign of God and helping people grasp an eternal reality and life that transcend everyday existence, this preaching seeks to empower people to endure the suffering of this world with hope and to live into the reality of God's coming reign, a way of life embodied by Christ's humility, generosity, unconditional love, and sacrifice.

A third way that preaching makes a heavenly connection with people is by assuring them that God loves them and will welcome them into heaven, even though they sin, doubt, rebel against God, and fail to live as God desires. As surely as all Christians know times when we ask Jesus what we must do to have eternal life, so all Christians know moments when, with the penitent thief on the cross, we plead, "Jesus, remember me when you come into your kingdom." We, too, long for the assurance that we will be with Jesus in paradise and that he has gone to prepare a place for us. Martin Luther asked whether we will encounter a judgmental or a merciful God in the hour of our death and found his answer in Paul's proclamation that, because we have been pronounced free from guilt by Christ's blood, how "much more will we be saved through him from the wrath of God."[11] Others find the assurance they need in Paul's proclamation that nothing can separate us from the love of Christ, or in Jesus's own declaration, "And I, when I am lifted up from the earth, will draw all people to myself."[12] This kind of sermon might note that, when Jesus preached in Nazareth, he skipped over the part of the reading from Isaiah that talked about the day of the Lord's vengeance. The message of this type of preaching is that, in the end, we are saved by God's unconditional love in Jesus Christ, rather than anything we do or fail to do. These sermons endeavor to relieve people from their fear that God will reject them if they fail to be worthy of God's love, so that they are free to try to live as Christ's people and, when they fail, to trust in God's mercy and try again.

Internal

Connie is not certain how she connects preaching and her daily life. All Connie knows is that something in sermons can touch her soul in a way that makes her want to be a better Christian. "It's like when Jesus said, 'Follow me' to the disciples," Connie reflects. "Something touched them inside and made them get up and leave their nets." For Connie that "something" might be the assurance that God loves her, but it also might be a word of challenge or correction. "Fear doesn't work, and neither does shame," Connie muses. "Mostly, it's gratitude. Sermons can make me feel so grateful for what God has done for us in Christ, and what God is doing in church and to make the world better, that I just want to be part of it."

We can call that "something" in preaching, which touches people's inner selves and causes them to live differently, the movement of the Holy Spirit or the power of Christ at work in the gospel. Teresa Fry Brown describes it as the "positive charge" of the word of God, which stimulates a change in people's negative charge—lack of faith, doubting faith, or need to reinforce personal belief—by introducing faith, acceptance, or belief.[13] Perhaps listeners are feeling poor, captive, and oppressed, and Jesus's declaration of good news, release, and freedom is fulfilled in their soul. Regardless of how we name it, preachers and listeners like Connie are convinced that, through preaching, God transforms people from the inside out, as something happens inside the believer so that she or he is different and better after the sermon.

Preachers and listeners like Connie consider the reign of God as something more than a coming attraction. God's reign happens all around us in ways we can see with the eyes of faith. Sermons can help believers see God's kingdom in our midst by pointing out the places and the ways God is bringing it—in our lives, in the church, and in the world. But, for these Christians, the focus of preaching is on spiritual matters, not changing the world. These Christians understand that the church's role in the reign of God is to create, preserve, and deepen faith. God works through other institutions and structures, including the family, education, the economy, and government, to order society, promote justice, and care for the afflicted and needy. Were these Christians to hear the sermon that Jesus preached at the synagogue in Nazareth, they would likely assume that Jesus was preaching about spiritual afflictions. After all, while the congregation certainly ministers to those who fall through the cracks, these Christians believe that religion and politics, church and state, ought to be kept separate. Experience teaches them that, when preachers talk about faith as something other than an individual, private matter, people take sides and things get contentious. As they see it, issues are never as clear-cut as the preacher makes them out to be, and often get in the way of preaching the gospel. Rather than risk jeopardizing people's faith and keeping them away from church, it is far better to preach in ways that stir people to live as Christians and love their neighbor and to trust God to change the world.

Individual

"For me, it's never as easy as the sermon moving me to be a better Christian, because life is rarely as neat as God working through the church to bring faith and society to bring order," Audrey said. "I need sermons that help me know how to be a better Christian in a really messy world. I'm not worried as much about how to get to heaven as I am about how to get through next week." Audrey views the separation of the church and other social structures as an indication of the brokenness in life; the world is not what God intends it to be. As Audrey attempts to negotiate this brokenness and live in a way that is in keeping with the coming reign of God, she frequently experiences tension and even conflict between her calling as a Christian and the realities of life and the ways of the world. Audrey desires preaching that connects with her life by helping her live with the tensions and faithfully make her way in the world. For Audrey, a sermon on Jesus's inaugural sermon would help her understand how Jesus can say "today" and "fulfilled" when people are still poor, blind, captive, and oppressed.

Audrey and those who share this perspective are convinced that Christians have a responsibility to be good citizens of this world by supporting and participating in God's work in and through society's institutions and structures. At the same time, as citizens of God's reign, Christians are compelled to speak out against and resist structures, systems, individuals, and institutions that are contrary to God's reign and stand in its way. For these Christians, how one walks this tightrope is a matter of individual conscience, personal choice, and prayerful discernment, because belonging to a faith community does not commit everyone to think or act the same way. Believers may bond together on certain issues, but they are not compelled to do so. Moreover, the church by its very nature moves slowly. The fast pace of life and the urgency of the issues we face often makes it impossible to wait for the church or even the congregation to reach unanimity or even consensus on what constitutes a faithful response. Faithful individuals must act as individuals. An individual gesture or witness to the reign of God can engender hope, motivate others to act or witness, and allow faith to inform if not govern the decisions people make.[14]

These Christians look to preaching to bring the resources of their faith and their individual beliefs to bear on the issues of their lives and of the world. They appreciate sermons that offer meaningful and practical help with issues they consider most important. For these Christians, sermons should address people's concerns, helping them to make sense of life. Preachers need to be aware of and respond to people's needs. The preacher might even diagnose those needs and attempt to treat them with the gospel by assessing what parts of the gospel message hearers need at this moment, and what parts of the gospel they can receive amid the pain and clutter of their lives. No topic is off-limits in preaching, because God is in it all. When the church claims that God is omnipresent, which means that God is eternally everywhere, regardless of whether we are aware of God's presence, the church asserts that no subject, issue, situation, or experience is beyond God's concern and unrelated to the church's proclamation of the gospel. Raising any issue or question from the pulpit should, therefore, be safe as long as the person doing so is sincere and respectful and grounds the issue in the proclamation of the gospel.[15]

Some listeners, like Drew, want absolutes, and some preachers want to provide them. They desire purity, draw sharp ideological boundaries, and want to avoid the evils of the fallen world, even as they seek to relate to it. They find diversity of beliefs and competing values systems, which characterize contemporary life, disconcerting and react against them by striving to preserve their traditional beliefs and Christian identity.[16] They fear that the comfort and assurance they receive from knowing their lives are part of the well-ordered providence of God are being replaced with the anxiety that faith claims are not as secure as they once had been. These Christians want the church to tell them how to live their lives. In a sense, they hold the church responsible for preserving their faith, protecting their worldview, and providing order in the chaos and confusion of daily life. They look to the church and its leaders to protect and guide, to warn and correct, by teaching the beliefs and practices that must be obeyed and defended.

Other Christians, like Audrey, connect preaching and their daily lives individually, but in another way. These listeners are convinced that, beyond the unchanging gospel of God's unconditional love and goodwill for us and all creation revealed in Jesus Christ, life is rarely neat enough for absolute beliefs and behaviors. Rather than pronouncing absolutes, these Christians look to the church's preaching to equip them to live in ways that take the gospel seriously. They appreciate sermons that provide tools that help them determine for themselves how to live as citizens of both the world and God's reign. They look to preaching to bring the gospel to bear on their lives in ways that model and empower them to reflect theologically for themselves and then to act accordingly. This kind of preaching requires both input and response from the listeners. Rather than eliminating tension and conflict, this preaching helps people address the internal and external conflict they experience as they try to reconcile their faith with conflicting values and realities and their religion with policies that contradict what the gospel claims and teaches.

Congregational

Lisa, who chairs the congregation's outreach committee, asked to meet with the preaching discussion group because she had some ideas about how to improve the congregation's preaching. The group resoundingly responded that the group's purpose is not to improve but to discuss preaching. If Lisa was interested in sharing what she finds meaningful in sermons, with no other agenda, they would be happy to have her join them. When the group gathered, Lisa explained that she gets excited by sermons that help the congregation be more mission minded. Lisa talked about another congregation she once belonged to. The congregation had a vision for mission and the pastor regularly preached on it. Every Sunday, right before the benediction, the congregation recited their vision statement. Together, they embodied and expressed their Christian values. They carried out a mission. They expressed their faith in action. Lisa sees Jesus giving a vision for mission to the church in Nazareth and inviting the congregation to be part of it.

Lisa and Christians like her value preaching that shapes the congregation's common life by grounding congregational action in the proclamation of the gospel. They look for sermons to connect to their lives and the life of the congregation by directing, positioning, and inspiring the members of the congregation to act together. They appreciate preaching that seeks to put communal energies to work. In response to the gospel, the preacher calls the people to live lives of thanksgiving *within the faith community*. "Acting in faith, the congregation does not wait for the resolution of complex issues, but sees a need and uses its meager resources to meet it."[17] To be effective, this preaching cannot be manipulative, coercive, or exclusionary. It addresses the people as a congregation rather than confirming or challenging individual ways.

Sermons intended to connect to the congregation as a whole and energize it for mission are often based on an image around which the congregation can rally and a simple, memorable message from which the congregation can act. Often the congregation takes its image and message from Scripture. The preacher uses the images and message to explain the biblical or theological foundation of the congregation's vision and what God is calling the congregation to do and be. The congregation may even choose to use sermons to clarify the particular activities the congregation will undertake to carry out its mission in its neighborhood or region. By regularly and repeatedly incorporating the vision into sermons, the preacher keeps the congregation's mission before the people and reinforces what they are called to do and be. People often respond positively to this preaching because of their relationship with their pastor and with congregation members with whom they share the life of faith.

Societal-Global

"My problem with discussing how we hope sermons will connect with our lives," Fred was thinking out loud, "is that the focus is on us. It may be on us individually; it may be on us as a congregation. But it's still all about us. I want sermons about God, about what God is doing in the world, and how we might connect with that. We keep talking about Jesus's sermon in Nazareth. Jesus preaches that today, here and now: he *is* releasing the captive, restoring the sight of those who are blind, announcing news that makes the poor rejoice, declaring the Lord's favor, and skipping over the part about God's vengeance. I want to connect with that, and I want preaching that helps me know how."

Fred and Christians like him, both preachers and listeners to sermons, resist anything that appears to relegate God to a specific sphere of life. For these Christians, God is more than omnipresent;

God stands center stage in everything, creating, sustaining, and renewing all things. These Christians understand that, in his sermon in Nazareth, Jesus inaugurates a revolutionary movement that will transform this world economically, socially, and politically. For Christians like Fred, faith is bigger than church. To have faith in Christ is to participate in God's activity in and purpose for creation, "a future beyond all human projection and imagining,"[18] and not merely to meet the needs of individuals or the congregation. Sermons attempt to help the congregation discern God's purpose for creation and how God calls the congregation to participate in it. More than welcoming any issue in preaching, these Christians insist that the church is obliged by faith to address from the pulpit every important issue confronting the world. While the ultimate response to the gospel is trust in God, to whom the future belongs, rather than in human action, trust in God compels the church to act individually and corporately to participate in God's future.

For these Christians, God frequently calls the church to act in ways that are countercultural and prophetic. However, because God's purpose for creation and the church's role in it are rarely unambiguous, the congregation's first responsibility is to be a place of education and discussion of issues based on the Bible, the congregation's confessional and theological heritage, and the resources of the Christian tradition. In other words, the congregation examines the issues confronting society, the family of nations, humanity, and the planet from the perspective of the gospel. In preaching, the church confronts biblical texts and interprets them in light of these issues, even as it interprets the issues in light of biblical texts. Preaching also provides a forum to wrestle with the issues by hearing one another's views and perhaps changing our own or someone else's opinion. The proclamation of our common faith and Christian identity also furnishes a place around which opposing interests can unite and be in harmony, even as they struggle to come to a consensus on positions and actions. Once the congregation decides on a course of action, preaching grounds that action theologically and calls for and empowers participation.

In one form or another, the congregation's words and deeds provide a prophetic and critical voice to the powers at work in the world when those powers run counter to the reign of God. The church names social wrongs and points to ways of addressing them. The church gives voice to the voiceless and brings their concerns into the public square. The church lifts up the needs of otherwise overlooked members of society, and calls society to respond to them. While some understand their mission as restoring a golden age, a return to basics and to the world they think they have lost,[19] most envision themselves as helping to build the city of God, which is nothing other than the restoration and fulfillment of the creation that God intends, which Jesus lived, died, and rose to inaugurate.

So how do you connect preaching and your daily life? The six possibilities I offered in this chapter are all applicable to individual Christians. Yet, living as Christians is more than an individual undertaking or a solo act. We live our Christian faith as part of a congregation or believing community. In the next chapter, I consider ways Christians relate to their congregations during preaching by considering why we sit where we do during the sermon.

Questions for Discussion

- How concerned is your congregation that sermons connect to people's lives? Do you think your congregation should change or strengthen this connection? How?
- Can congregations become so overly concerned with being relevant and getting results that this quest prevents that from happening? How can you tell when this is happening?
- Are there subjects or topics that should not be addressed from the pulpit? What are they?
- Read Luke 4:16-30. How does Jesus's sermon connect to your life? Why do you think Jesus's sermon didn't work?
- What is the prominent way that you connect preaching and your daily life? Can you sense how your congregation connects preaching and daily life?

Chapter Six

Why Do You Sit
Where You Do?

"What do you mean, why do we sit where we do?" The group stared blankly at Pastor Mark. "If the sermon was only about interacting with the preacher," Pastor Mark answered thoughtfully, "you'd all be sitting in the first few pews, right in front of the pulpit. So why do people sit in the back or in the balcony? Why do some members of our congregation sit together all bunched up, while others spread out and refuse to slide over, even when the place is packed? I think it has something to do with the way people interact with one another in worship."

Fred interrupted, "Isn't interacting with the congregation during the sermon something *you* are supposed to do?" Everyone laughed, but Pastor Mark wasn't giving in. "Audrey sits front and center, her eyes fixed on the pulpit, but Drew seems more interested in having a good view of the cross and stained glass than of me. Eleanor tells us that her Sunday school class looks everywhere except at the pulpit, and kids aren't the only ones." Looking over at Brian, Pastor Mark continued, "I like to look up at Brian in the balcony and catch him checking out the congregation during the sermon. And Eleanor, I'd like to be in on the running commentary that you and the church ladies are having in the back. So why do you sit where you do?"

Asking about where people choose to sit during the sermon and inviting them to become aware of the implications for that choice may at first appear to be a silly exercise, because it is not something most people ordinarily think about. Yet, reflecting on how people position themselves in relation to others during the sermon, and indeed throughout the entire worship service, provides important clues to how a congregation understands itself as a faith community and an expression of the church. Human behavior communicates meaning. Carefully observing and interpreting how people relate during an event as central to a congregation's life as the Sunday sermon provides insights into the character of their common life. People's interactions reveal how they order their world. Whether the nature of a congregation's common life is explicitly declared in a mission statement and consciously nurtured by its leaders or unconsciously expressed in the way the congregation worships together, the kind of faith community a congregation is has important implications for its mission. For example, congregations that desire to grow frequently have difficulty doing so, because having more members will change the way members interact, how decisions get made, and how the congregation understands itself as an expression of the church. Asking people to observe how they relate to other members of the congregation during important moments in their shared life, especially worship and preaching, can help congregations understand how they must change if they are to grow.

Yet, becoming aware of and reflecting on an interaction as simple as where we sit in church, and teasing out the implications of a congregation's seating arrangement, is not easy. First, everyone in a congregation rarely chooses their seats for the same reason, although some worshipers may appear to have made the same choice. Parents with energetic children choose the last pew for a different reason than the grieving widow sitting alone. But both make a decision about how they will interact with the congregation. Second, as people become conscious of why they sit where they do and how they act in worship, they may alter their behavior, particularly if they are embarrassed by what they are doing. Pastor Mark's comment to Eleanor might stop the church ladies' running commentary, at least for a while. Moreover, Christian worship is designed, in part, to alter people's behavior by bringing it more in step with the congregation's understanding of discipleship and Christian living. People may behave a certain way in church precisely because they are in church. A congregation that warmly huddles together at the coffee hour may sit straight, silent, and spread out during the worship service, because members have been taught that a quiet, formal disposition is appropriate for Christian worship. Finally, we need to be careful how we interpret others' behavior. Parishioners who, upon entering church, chat with those around them may intend to engage others in order to worship more fully as the body of Christ. However, they may be perceived by others as casual and even irreverent. Someone who closes his eyes and lowers his head during a sermon may be perceived as sleeping when he is, in fact, seriously concentrating. For members, a congregation sitting close together is warm and intimate; for visitors, the congregation may feel closed. Mindful of these cautions, we can be aware of and attempt to interpret how we interact with the congregation during worship and preaching by reflecting on why we choose to sit where we do.

Why observe where we sit during the sermon as opposed to some other aspect of congregational life, like the coffee hour? As part of the worship service, preaching is an activity in which we claim to be most aware of and committed to our identity as a faith community and the body of Christ. As I described in chapter 4, we all have expectations about how sermons ought to connect with us individually. Most Christians also hope preaching will cause or at least help something positive to happen in the life of the congregation as well. For example, Charles Campbell, who teaches preaching at Columbia Theological Seminary in Decatur, Georgia, argues that the purpose of preaching is to build up the community of faith as "a people who practice the way of God, as embodied in Jesus Christ, in and for the world."[1] Campbell observes that in the Sermon on the Mount, Jesus seeks to constitute the community of the disciples who will embody his way of life in the world. In this community, reconciliation takes priority over vengeance, women are not treated as objects or property, and love of enemies and nonviolent resistance replace violent domination. In the community that Jesus establishes, people do not use religious practices to build themselves up while tearing others down, and the desire for wealth is not the driving force of life.[2]

So how is preaching building up your congregation as a community of faith? In this chapter, I invite you to begin to find out by observing why you sit where you do during preaching and reflecting on what your choice of seats says about how you interact with members of your congregation during the sermon. In the introduction, I reported that some people regard the sermon as strictly an individual encounter. Others hope this individual encounter will also have an effect on the congregation, while yet others consider the sermon to be preached to the congregation as a community rather than a gathering of individuals. Perhaps you can gain insight beyond these generalizations by asking yourself, "Why do I sit where I do?" Are you aware that other people are there? Do you interact with them overtly or subtly, consciously or unconsciously, individually or as a group?

To help us answer this question, we turn to images of the church. The New Testament is filled with wonderful images for Christ's church. Among these images, the New Testament portrays Christ's church as a ripe harvest, the flock of the Good Shepherd, a ship sailing calmly through troubled seas, the family of Jesus, branches of the vine, a living temple, the bride of Christ the bridegroom, and the body of Christ.[3] Still, when asked what the church is, most people respond that the church is a place. "We go to church." Or, they will tell you that the church is a building. "There's the church. There's the steeple. Open the doors, and see all the people." So what kind of place is the church? What kinds of places emerge when we consider where members of a congregation sit during the sermon and why they choose their seats?

Figure 6.1. Where Do You Sit and Why?

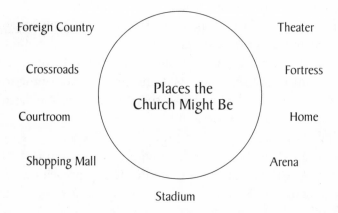

In this chapter I suggest nine places that a congregation might be, based on where people sit during sermons. A congregation might be a (1) foreign country, (2) shopping mall, (3) fortress, (4) courtroom, (5) theater, (6) home, (7) arena, (8) crossroads, and (9) stadium. My aim is to help congregations connect these places with the activity of the kingdom, reign, or commonwealth of God, so that worship and mission are indistinguishable, informing and flowing from each other. I will have more to say about the church's mission in chapter 7.

Foreign Country

Brian agreed with Pastor Mark that he spends much of the service, particularly the sermon, observing members of the congregation. Although Brian grew up going to church, he has been away a long while. While Brian was gone, things changed, or perhaps he did. For Brian, coming back to church was like crossing the border into a foreign country. Brian finds the worship service confusing. For Brian, religious jargon, like *kyrie* and *absolution*, is a foreign language. The congregation has customs and ways of acting that are unfamiliar and even strange to Brian. Pressed for a biblical image that describes the church, Brian reads God's command to Abraham: "Go from your country . . . to the land that I will show you."[4] The church is the land that God is showing Brian. Brian sits in the balcony, on the border of this foreign country, and watches members of the congregation in order to learn their language and customs. He observes people during the sermon to see how they are reacting to what Pastor Mark is saying. Brian then compares their reactions to the sermon with his own.

Brian also watches to see how members of the congregation welcome and treat those who cross the border into their country. At St. Ambrose Church, people greet visitors and make a point to talk to them at the coffee fellowship following the service. If visitors have questions or need assistance, the members of St. Ambrose Church are more than willing to help. At the same time, the congregation has its way of worshiping, and visitors pretty much need to figure it out for themselves. Helpful directions are provided in the worship folder and some members will offer a hand if visitors look as though they are having trouble following along. But members are cautious, for fear of insulting someone. Pastor Mark usually explains religious language when he uses it in sermons and uses illustrations most people can relate to. Yet, a certain familiarity with the gospel, the Bible, and the Christian faith is presumed. Brian is okay with this, because he believes that it takes time to go from being a tourist to a visitor to a citizen of a country. Brian appreciates that the people of St. Ambrose Church give him the time and space he needs to get comfortable. They answer his questions, give him the help he asks for, and do not seem to mind when he gets things wrong or makes a mistake. Brian has talked a couple times at St. Ambrose with people who have indicated they are new to the church or have also been away for a long time. He has noticed that after a while, most of them quit coming back. He can't help but wonder whether they found the experience too foreign and sometimes thinks about whether the congregation could reach out to these folks. He remembers a sermon Pastor Mark preached about welcoming the orphan, the widow, and the sojourner[5] and wonders if crossing the border is just too hard for them.

Shopping Mall

Brian ran into one of these acquaintances in a coffee shop. He told Brian about a congregation that responds differently to people who experience the church as a foreign country and venture across the border into worship. This congregation, New Day Christian Church, tries to eliminate the border altogether. No one sits in the balcony because the border is right in front of the stage. At New Day, the business of Sunday morning is to welcome visitors and meet their needs. This congregation lifts up as an image of the church Jesus's parable of the great dinner, in which the master sent slaves into the roads and lanes to compel people to come in, so that the master's house may be filled.[6] These Christians remind us that, as I discussed in chapter 1, Jesus preached beside the sea, in the marketplace, and wherever he could gather a crowd. Their approach is to emulate Jesus's ministry, so that going to church is as comfortable as going to the mall. Newcomers will not sit on the edges because they feel welcome and comfortable in every seat in the house.

Congregations like New Day Church may even worship in buildings that look like malls, with a coffee bar, bookstore, and professionally staffed child-care center. Traditional Christian symbols are removed from the worship space, which resembles an auditorium. Parking lot attendants both help people find a place to park and greet them with a smile. Ushers and greeters welcome people in ways that make them feel safe and help them relax and open up. The host and hostess at coffee fellowship guarantee that visitors have someone to talk with. Signs tell people the locations of restrooms, nursery, and Sunday school. Rovers in worship spot visitors and sit with and assist them.

Worship is designed to convey warmth, friendliness, and acceptance. The worship leader assumes that people have never been to church before and so announces and explains everything. Sermons present the gospel, Bible, and Christian faith as completely new. Religious language is replaced with the language of the culture. People go to church for the same reason they go to the mall—to get what they need. Preaching, therefore, is designed so that everyone gets something out of every sermon. To ensure that the needs of every individual in worship are met, congregations often become a "specialty store" by identifying a "target audience." The congregation might, for example, actively seek to attract white, middle-class, socially progressive suburbanites. The assumption is that this homogenous group of people is emotionally and intellectually in the same place, concerned with the same things, and holds similar ideas. Preaching, worship, and congregational programs are designed to appeal to this specific audience. People who do not fit into this homogenous group are entrusted to another faith community. People are not expected to actively interact with one another in worship, because that might make them uncomfortable. Rather, the focus in worship is on interacting with the preacher and musicians, personal and individual relationships with God, and membership in the congregation, which often involves commitment to a small group.

Fortress

While the people of New Day Church open themselves up to people like a shopping mall, other congregations seem to lock themselves down like a fortress. The psalmist declares, "The LORD is my rock, my fortress . . . my stronghold."[7] Some Christians and congregations so cherish this image of God that they want the church to be a fortress as well. Often, these congregations preserve their sense of safety and stability by resisting any change. "Jesus Christ is the same yesterday and today and forever"[8] might be their mission statement. Confronted by the uncertainties and complexities of life, all Christians can appreciate this yearning.

People sit in "their" pew, where they have always sat, even when the congregation is tiny and the worship space is cavernous. The worship service is "as we've always done it," which means that it has not changed for as long as anyone can remember; worship often includes peculiar practices that the congregation assumes are normal and even universal. Preserving peace and stability are the congregation's priorities, even if that means putting up with idiosyncratic behavior. To maintain the harmony of their fortress, members fall into line behind whatever needs to happen.

The members of the congregation look for preaching to reinforce their group identity and contribute to their peace and stability. Perhaps even more than the quality of preaching, they appreciate hearing the sermon with the same people they have worshiped with for years. During the sermon, worshipers may interact with each other about the preacher more than they interact with the preacher, because it takes them a long time to stop regarding the preacher as an outsider to the group. Until they come to trust the preacher, these congregations value preaching when the sermon's form is predictable, its theology is traditional, the message is about God's steadfast love and faithfulness, and the goal is to reassure and reinforce rather than to challenge or disrupt the status quo. In sermons, contemporary life and even the greater church furnish the foes from which the congregation needs protection.

When it comes to visitors, these congregations appear to post guards at the border. Greeters are replaced by doorkeepers, whose unspoken job is to ascertain who visitors are, why they are there, what they want, and what, if anything, they can offer the congregation. Often, the congregation is suspicious of visitors who are different from its members. Everything about the congregation, from which church door is unlocked to the location of restrooms to the stories the preacher tells in sermons, seems to be inside information. Members have designated spaces in the parking lot and pews in the worship space, and members let visitors know when they are in them. Members talk to each other at the coffee fellowship, leaving visitors standing against the wall or at the fringes of conversation rather than sitting at the table. Interacting with members of the congregation is hard for visitors because, while members will whisper to each other about visitors, they are uncomfortable talking to visitors directly.

Courtroom

"A congregation with doorkeepers sounds to me like a courtroom," Drew laughed. Then, after a long pause, he added, "Sometimes, that's how I feel when I come to church, like I'm going to court." Drew likes to sit where he can look at the cross and stained-glass windows as he listens to Pastor Mark preach about sin and how Jesus died for us. Occasionally, as Drew takes in the beautiful sanctuary during the sermon, he understands how the prophet Isaiah felt when he saw the Lord sitting on a high and lofty throne, attended by six-winged seraphs.[9] Drew knows himself to be "a man of unclean lips" and, looking around during the sermon, he sees that everyone else knows it too, about him and about themselves. The congregation is "a people of unclean lips." Pastor Mark does not attack them in the sermon; he is a witness in this courtroom, testifying about them and about himself, and God is the judge. God does not find them innocent. God pardons them for Jesus's sake.

Looking around during sermons, Drew also sees that, sometimes, he and the other members of the congregation are not the accused. They are the jury. On those occasions, the sermon is a trial between the claims of the gospel and the other claims that so fill our lives and the world. After talking with Brian, Drew decided that visitors, in particular, are jurors. Visitors judge the congregation according to its stated beliefs. When the sermon is a trial between competing claims, the congregation is marked by struggle and divergent opinions. Worship sometimes feels as though opposing values and even lives are at stake. It felt that way to Drew on the Sunday that Pastor Mark preached about the Parson family and the council of churches' appeal to give them money. Looking around the congregation, Drew noticed that people did not seem to agree with Pastor Mark that we are all forgiven sinners, at least not to the same degree. In Drew's estimation, people resented having their sin equated with what Rev. Parson allegedly did. It seemed to Drew that, at the meeting after church, the congregation resonated with other values that preserved their individuality.

Drew also knows that at times the sermon provides an occasion to observe others in worship, including Pastor Mark, to see how well their lives and actions correspond to the word of God, particularly as that word is spoken from the pulpit. Occasionally, Drew catches himself feeling like the Pharisee in Jesus's parable about the Pharisee and the tax collector, thanking God he is not like other people.[10] At other times, Drew feels like the tax collector. Drew thinks that people sometimes put the entire congregation on trial—for example, Eleanor, who he thinks judged the entire congregation for not extending forgiveness. Drew knows that many people feel Lisa judges the congregation for lack of mission. Drew, who in his heart mostly feels unworthy, is concerned that the congregation worship "correctly" and gets nervous and frustrated when mishaps happen, particularly when worship leaders appear unprepared or unengaged.

Theater

"Now I'm feeling a bit silly," Audrey said. "I don't really pay attention to the people sitting around me during the sermon. I approach a sermon the same way I do a movie at the theater. And I know pastors who preach as if they are on stage. 'The show must go on!' The sermon goes on regardless of the congregation."

People who pick their seat in church as they pick their seat at the theater often approach the sermon as a performance. Rather than looking at each other, people pay attention to what is happening up front. They want preaching, worship, and music that are aesthetically pleasing, as well as meaningful. While members of the congregation may occasionally respond to the sermon together, for example by laughing at a joke, most often they remain quiet so as not to disturb those sitting around them. Some congregations reinforce this theater experience by dimming the lights in the nave, so that members of the congregation cannot see each other, and shining a spotlight on the preacher. When the congregation functions like an audience at the theater, people experience the sermon individually, although with others who share the same space. Perhaps that is how the crowd experienced the apostles' preaching on Pentecost, when "each one heard them speaking in the native language of each."[11]

For people who participate in sermons as they do a play or movie, preaching can only build up the community indirectly. In worship, preaching can inspire the congregation to act together. Just as a play or concert can cause an audience to rise together and give a standing ovation, so a sermon can lead a congregation to join their voices in song and their hearts in prayer. While people may have experienced the sermon individually, they respond as part of the audience. After the worship service is over, the congregation often talks about the sermon in the same manner that an audience discusses a play or movie after having seen it. This conversation occurs at the coffee fellowship after worship and at other times and places during the week when members of the congregation get together. Sermons build up the congregation when they give people something to think about and discuss and when they provide an emotional experience, such as a moving story, that people can reflect upon and share.

Congregations that function like a theater work very well for people who want to come to worship but do not want to participate in other areas of a congregation's life. Worshipers can function as individuals, whether engaging in polite conversation before and after worship or choosing to remain anonymous, and still

participate in the service in meaningful ways. Those who desire
a greater experience of community find it in the congregation's
fellowship, education, and service activities. Congregations sometimes get frustrated by newcomers who approach the church as a
theater, when they are slow to volunteer or to become involved in
the congregation beyond worship. Even when worship attendance
increases, the congregation's volunteer base may not grow, leaving
the same people to do everything.

Home

Connie considers St. Ambrose Church her spiritual home and the
congregation her church family. Jesus says, "Whoever does the will
of my Father in heaven is my brother and sister and mother,"[12] and
Connie has found Jesus's family among the people of St. Ambrose.
They worship together, pray for each other, and care for one another when they are sick or in trouble. They also laugh together,
study the Bible together, share potluck suppers, and volunteer together in their community. Members see each other at the store
and at school activities. They visit in one another's homes. Some
of them really are family. That is why Connie finds it difficult to
imagine joining another church.

For people like Connie who consider the church their home,
where they sit in worship is not as important as who they are sitting with. The congregation is a family with whom they share a
common life. Preaching builds up the family when it speaks to
this common life. Sermons that address people or realities beyond
the congregation and local community are less helpful. The style
and content of sermons often vary. As a family, the congregation
feels interconnected, like the body of Christ. Members realize that
some weeks the sermon will address them directly. The message
will relate to them personally, and the form of the sermon will be
one they appreciate. Other weeks, the sermon's form and message
will relate directly to other members of the family. In fact, people
often think of and glance over at those members as they listen to
sermons. The congregation does not use a standard form of worship. Rather, the congregation has found a form and style that

work for the family. While not everyone appreciates everything in the service, everyone finds something to appreciate in the service and knows someone who really appreciates the things they don't. The congregation is content to take turns having sermons directly relate to them, because they know that every sermon relates to someone in the family and rejoice that people they deeply care about are receiving the gospel. These days, Connie just wishes that her turn would come a bit more often.

People who consider the church their home sometimes assume that everyone in the family—and even the whole world—shares their values. As in many families, certain things are left unspoken, certain subjects are taboo, and some realities are left unaddressed. The congregation often takes great pride in its physical home; when a need or an expense arises, someone always takes care of it. This leaves some members frustrated because there are never money and volunteers for ministries. The close-knit family circle, which these congregations often consider to be their greatest strength, can become a real barrier to visitors. While the congregation may sincerely desire new members and work very hard to welcome them, the congregation's interconnectedness still makes it hard for visitors to feel at home. After all, even in homes where guests are treated extremely well, it takes time and effort to become part of the family. To offset this reality, sermons challenge the church family not to turn in on itself but instead to seek to be a home for all people.

Arena

"I think of the church as an arena," Fred declared. "I'd call the church a wrestling ring, but that's too masculine." The group responded with puzzled looks, so Fred launched into the story of Jacob wrestling with an angel. "Remember how Jacob connived with his mother to steal his brother Esau's birthright? Remember how shrewdly he swindled his father-in-law out of a flock of fine sheep? His name, Jacob, literally means 'cheat,' and this name is well deserved. We find the cheat on his way home for a family reunion with brother Esau. What do you suppose Jacob is longing for alone in the night? What Jacob gets is a long night of struggle with an unnamed assailant. Jacob also gets a new identity. No longer 'cheat,' he is the one 'who strives with God.' Jacob limps away into a new life. Visited by the unnamed presence of God, he is a different person. The 'cheat' ends up playing a decisive role in God's purpose. And isn't that just like God to choose to wrestle a cheat into God's service?"

Fred continued, "I think that's what happens to us in church. We're not sitting; we're wrestling. God wrestles with us as we listen to the sermon. We are rebellious people. Like Jacob, we prefer our schemes to God's will, and we certainly don't want to be reconciled with our brothers and sisters. But God pins us down and changes who we are. And God doesn't yield. Unseen but unceasing, God reshapes our lives. Some weeks, the struggle is agonizing, even crippling, but God frees us from ourselves. Wounded, less self-confident, we emerge whole."

Fred thinks of the church as an arena where people come to seriously struggle with God, knowing their life depends upon it. People are not in the stands; they are in the center ring. For Fred, preaching is nothing other than the congregation wrestling with God. As the Scriptures are read and as they are preached, God speaks to the congregation as God's people, leaving the congregation to struggle with what God's word of grace means for its life and for the life of the world. Preaching builds up the community when the gospel is proclaimed in a way that forces the congregation to struggle together about the issues confronting them and the world. More than asking God for help and direction, sermons help members ask themselves, one another, and God what God is calling them to do and be in this time and place. As far as Fred is concerned, people should not talk about the sermon after the service; they should continue the conversation that the sermon started.

When the church is an arena in which Christians struggle and question God, get pinned down and blessed, emerge wounded but whole, less self-confident but somehow new, what goes on in church is a people witnessing to and participating in God's reconciling love for the world. As they struggle together with God, congregations claim those traits of God, their common life, and the work to which God calls them in such a way that they remain steadfast and discern together what God calls them to believe and do in this time and place. Because God's will and direction are never completely knowable, a congregation's struggle with God is constant. These congregations seek to be a safe place where visitors can bring their own struggles into God's presence and join in the congregation's ongoing wrestling with God. Of course, wrestling with God can be scary and unsettling. Struggling with God can make going to church feel unsafe and cause some people, both members and visitors, to stay away. The struggle can also get sidetracked by people pushing their own agendas. The challenge for congregations is to struggle with God together rather than wrestling each other.

Crossroads

"I'd like to take out the pews!" Lisa declared. "Jesus said, 'Then people will come from east and west, from north and south, and will eat in the kingdom of God.'"[13] Lisa envisions the fullness of God's reign as a great crossroads, where all people from the ends of the earth come together as the body of Christ, united in God's love. At this great crossroads, people of different languages, ethnicities, personality types, educational backgrounds, economic and social locations, and life experiences find more than unity or common ground. They find a synergy; gathered by the Holy Spirit, acting together as the body of Christ, they become something greater than they are apart from Christ and one another.

For Lisa, the pews get in the way of St. Ambrose congregation's mission as an expression of Christ's church to serve as a sign, God's token, pledge and promise of this coming reality. When the congregation gathers for worship, people come from many different places with many different perspectives. Through worship and preaching, the Holy Spirit gathers all those who come to church and forms them as the body of Christ for service in the world. The congregation's worship is itself a crossroads in that it is a prototype and preview of the fullness of the reign of God. Visitors are welcomed for the new perspectives they bring, which enrich the congregation. Lisa points out that people taking a seat, rather than standing together, keeps that from happening. She prays that more people of greater diversity will become part of the congregation, so that its worship will increasingly be a witness to and participation in God's coming reign.

Preaching at the crossroads calls for more than sensitivity to the diversity of the congregation, though this sensitivity is most certainly essential. Preaching at the crossroads invites a congregation to do more than to struggle together with the word of grace proclaimed in the sermon. Preaching at the crossroads builds up the congregation as the body of Christ by providing "the literal speaking and learning center of the church."[14] First and most important, the sermon proclaims the gospel of Jesus Christ. As part of or a consequence of this gospel proclamation, the sermon then gives voice to the diverse individuals, groups, and perspectives that are part of the congregation, as well as those individuals, groups, and perspectives that, while not physically present, are nonetheless part of the communion of saints. In this way, preaching builds up the congregation as an expression of the coming reign of God by providing an opportunity for all who gather to hear and understand each other and to encounter the gospel from people's diverse backgrounds, experiences, and perspectives. In this way, the congregation witnesses to and proclaims that God's love, revealed in Jesus Christ, transcends, embraces, and sanctifies all people and all creation.

Stadium

"I think the reason I'm so disappointed by the way our church responded to the Parson family appeal," Eleanor said, "is that I come to church to be part of something bigger and better than myself." As the Epistle to the Hebrews suggests, Eleanor comes to worship so that others can help her hold on to her confession of hope, to be provoked (and to provoke others) to love and do good deeds, and so that she and the other members of the congregation can encourage each other. Eleanor comes to worship to be surrounded by that great cloud of witnesses of which the author of Hebrews writes.[15]

Eleanor imagines the church as a great stadium. The congregation takes the field surrounded by the saints who faithfully persevered, gloriously triumphed, and now cheer the congregation on to victory. The congregation runs onto the field behind Jesus, who endured the cross, rose from the dead, sits at God's right hand, and is present among the members of the congregation as they worship.

For Eleanor, interacting with the members of the congregation is the point of worship and preaching. She sits in the back so that she can see the congregation. She whispers to her friends about the sermon because she is certain someone would have a heart attack if she talked back to Pastor Mark. Eleanor's favorite part of the service is sharing the peace. She wants the liturgy, prayers, hymns, and the other parts of the service to function like cheers, bands, and the wave in a real stadium. They transform a mass of individuals into a power with a corporate identity that transcends people's individual identities. In worship, everyone is first and foremost a child of God.

Eleanor desires preaching that celebrates this identity and helps the faith community understand and experience itself as part of the church of all times and places, the communion of saints, Christ's body in the world. The preacher might consciously address the congregation as a single community rather than as a gathering of individuals. Sermons might be designed to facilitate interaction through the use of direct questions, invitations to turn to a neighbor, or calls for an audible response. Most important, sermons should do more than proclaim the gospel. Sermons should themselves be an experience of the grace and power of the gospel active in the congregation and a celebration of faith, praise, and thanksgiving for God's love in Jesus Christ that leads the congregation to join in with one voice.

When this happens, worship is an in-breaking and an appetizer of what awaits us when Christ gathers the church of all times and places to himself. Eleanor imagines that, as more and more people take to the field, the walls of the stadium get pushed out farther and farther, until worship in church and life in the world are one and the same. In this stadium, the distinction between member and visitor disappears as all are together in God's presence. Then, as the writer of Revelation says, "I saw no temple in the city, for its temple is the Lord God the Almighty and the Lamb."[16]

"Okay," Lisa said, "sermons build up the congregation as a whole, as well as individual members. But can we talk about what preaching builds the congregation up to do and be?" Lisa had returned to her question about the relationship of preaching and mission. That relationship is determined, in part, by how the congregation understands the church's mission. You and I will consider this question in chapter 7. However, before we talk about what we are supposed to do when we get up from our seats and leave worship, spend some time discussing why you sit where you do.

Questions for Discussion

- During a sermon, be conscious of how you interact with other members of the congregation. What do you notice? What, if anything, would you like to change? How would your relationship to the congregation change if you sat somewhere else?
- Are sermons addressed to individuals, a gathering of individuals, or a single community? How can you tell?
- How are children permitted to act during worship? What behaviors are considered inappropriate and even unacceptable? What is the congregation teaching about how one interacts with the sermon?
- Are there congregational norms for how one enters worship, chooses a seat, responds to a sermon, prays, or receives the Lord's Supper? What are they?
- Where do visitors sit? How would visitors to your congregation describe the way they are welcomed and how members of the congregation interact with them?
- Which place depicted in this chapter best describes how you perceive your congregation as it worships?

Chapter Seven

How Should We Respond to Sermons?

"We just need to become more mission minded," Lisa told Pastor Mark as the two entered the church library, where the preaching group met. "What is our vision for mission?" Lisa is truly concerned that lack of attention to, not to mention enthusiasm for, mission and evangelism are chronic problems for the people of St. Ambrose Church. Lisa acknowledges that overall the members of the congregation take their faith very seriously. Both as individuals and as a faith community, they welcome visitors and are involved in their neighborhood and the greater community. While no one considers St. Ambrose Church politically active, it is known for being concerned with issues of justice and ministering to those in need. But the congregation is slow to embrace what Lisa understands to be Jesus's Great Commission—making disciples of all nations and teaching them to observe all that Jesus commands. People do not tell others about Jesus, they say, because evangelism is not their gift. Like many Christians, they equate evangelism with the Crusades, telemarketing, confrontation, and intimidation, and so they do not invite their friends to church. They resist talking to other members of the church about why those members do not attend worship regularly, participate in Bible study, or tithe. Most members of the congregation are embarrassed when, in Christian love, Lisa suggests to people how they can grow in faith and discipleship. The congregation does not seem interested in changing its ways to attract more people. Lisa wishes that Pastor Mark would preach about the church's mission more frequently and has repeatedly urged him to do so.

"Not another visioning process," someone groaned as Pastor Mark and Lisa took their seats. The group laughed, then sighed.

"I think the reason we have trouble coming up with a vision that sticks," Pastor Mark said, "is not that we don't care about mission. I don't think we've come to a consensus about what the church's mission is."

"The church's mission is clear to me," Lisa retorted. "It's in the Bible. Jesus said, 'Go therefore and make disciples of all nations.'"

Brian interrupted. "If you tried to make me a disciple when I came back to church, I'd have bolted."

"Like I said," Pastor Mark attempted to relieve the growing tension in the room. "We may not all be comfortable with this way of understanding the church's mission. The question we need to ask is, what vision for mission most fully captures what we believe God is calling us to do?"

"I wonder," Fred asked, "in Scripture, is the Great Commission the only thing Jesus told the disciples to do?" The members of the group assumed Fred already knew the answer to his question, so they started flipping through their Bibles, looking for other "commissions." They discovered that the Great Commission is not the only farewell instructions from Jesus recorded in Scripture. In fact, in the New Testament, Jesus commissioned the church to do many things. Pastor Mark suggested that the next time the group meets, each member share a commission or command from Jesus that speaks to and excites them.

Figure 7.1. How Should We Respond to Sermons?

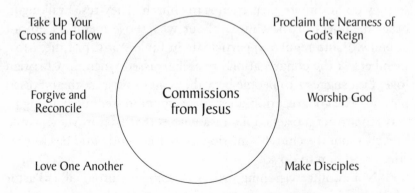

Take Up Your
Cross and Follow

Proclaim the Nearness of
God's Reign

Forgive and
Reconcile

Commissions
from Jesus

Worship God

Love One Another

Make Disciples

The next time the group met, Lisa was still eager to talk about (1) making disciples. Other members shared passages in which Jesus commands his followers to (2) take up their cross and follow; (3) forgive and reconcile; (4) worship God; (5) love one another; and (6) proclaim the nearness of God's reign. These and many other scriptural charges are certainly variations on a common theme. In chapter 1, I described the vision that guided Jesus's preaching ministry as "fulfillment." As the extension of Jesus's preaching ministry, the church lives by and exists for the proclamation of the gospel. Jesus appointed and trained preachers to continue his ministry and sent them out to proclaim the same gospel that Jesus himself preached. Jesus extended his own preaching ministry by empowering and authorizing the apostles, and after them the church, to preach in his name. Moreover, the responsibility to proclaim the gospel is not limited to a particular office; Jesus entrusts the proclamation of the gospel to every Christian and the entire church.

Regardless of how it defines its mission, a congregation's reason for being is to alert the world to the fulfillment of God's promises in Jesus Christ and to the implications of the good news for people's lives and for the world. Yet, Christians and congregations resonate with some variations of this common theme more than others. Congregations are more likely to embrace a mission that captures their imagination as a natural consequence of the gospel proclamation than one they perceive as a separate agenda they feel obliged to carry out. That said, rather than choosing one scriptural commission and dismissing the others, congregations are most likely to discern God's will for them when they prayerfully consider every biblical commission they can as they seek to connect their congregation with God's work of salvation. Pastor Mark's question might be restated as, "How should we respond to sermons?"

Make Disciples

Countless Christians and congregations join Lisa in revering the Great Commission as Jesus's personal, specific, and final instructions to all Christians and congregations. These instructions spell out what Christ calls the church to do—make disciples, baptize, and teach. Or, in the Gospel of Mark's terms, "proclaim the good news to the whole creation. The one who believes and is baptized will be saved."[1] The church is to boldly put its faith in action by going forth to make disciples. The church's mission to make disciples applies to all nations, all peoples, and all cultures. As part of this mission, the church is to carry on Jesus's teaching ministry, and Jesus's sermons, particularly the Sermon on the Mount, provide the content of the church's instruction. Jesus promises to be present with and support the church as it makes decisions, studies Scripture, prays, preaches, baptizes, and teaches.

Christians and congregations determining how they will fulfill the Great Commission involves prayer, discernment, and decision. Consequently, congregations and their leaders need to be concerned with defining the mission and equipping and empowering members to carry it out in ways appropriate to the congregation's specific context. In different congregations and denominations, the Great Commission provides the scriptural warrant for an abundance of ministries, including carrying out direct missionary work aimed at bringing the gospel to the entire world; providing leadership development, education, and technology in order to disciple all nations; furnishing leadership and oversight to developing churches; working to transform people's lives from poverty to plenty; and standing *with* those who suffer by standing *against* violence, oppression, and injustice. The Great Commission also provides the basis of Christian education and theological inquiry.

Many Christians and congregations find in the Great Commission the biblical basis for "growing" churches. These congregations name making disciples as their primary purpose. They have a passion for all who have no relationship with Christ and understand that, because the church is confronted by a changing world, the methods they use to convey the gospel need to change. They pray, "Lord, do whatever it takes," including setting aside a democratic process of decision making, which they regard as unbiblical, so that leaders can implement the mission. These congregations intentionally shake things up for the sake of growth and accept the reality that to be missional may mean losing longtime members. They give people choices in worship, education, fellowship, and other activities. Success—and sometimes faithfulness—is measured in terms of church growth, often measured by numbers of people in worship.

A congregation's specific vision for mission determines the content, form, and style of preaching. The vision is regularly the content of sermons for congregational members, whom the preacher entreats to become involved. Preaching to nonmembers often transmits information about Jesus. Teaching involves distinguishing between God and the world, the sacred and the profane, and defining how Christians behave differently from other people. Preaching is often directed to individuals; its aim is to help them decide for Christ, begin a relationship with Jesus, and become members of the congregation.

Take Up Your Cross

"I've been to churches where some of Jesus's teachings are emphasized more than others," Brian said. "Congregations generally don't disciple people in ways that won't help their church grow. For example, Jesus told his disciples, 'If any want to become my followers, let them deny themselves and take up their cross and follow me. For those who want to save their life will lose it, and those who lose their life for my sake will find it.' I think some churches downplay this teaching because they're not sure that it will help their church grow."[2]

Brian correctly observes that congregations committed to making disciples—and all congregations, really—sometimes have difficulty applying certain sayings of Jesus to themselves, because some of what Jesus teaches about discipleship undermines church growth. Preachers may apply Jesus's call to self-denial and cross bearing to individual Christians and invite them to embrace Christlike self-sacrifice for the sake of the congregation and its mission. However, for a host of reasons, chief of which is institutional survival, pastors do not ordinarily preach that Christ may be calling a congregation to lose its life for the sake of the gospel. Pastors and church leaders who regularly challenge members to tithe may not embrace that challenge communally by giving away a tithe of the congregation's income. All preachers struggle with how to wield the sword of Jesus's teaching without slicing the congregation to pieces. Openness to self-sacrifice; sharing patiently in affliction; resisting the lure of power, influence, and status; and refusing to compete according to the rules of the world, all of which Jesus modeled on the cross, are not visions for mission that attract new members and grow churches. Perhaps this is why few congregations embrace them.

Sermons that treat Jesus's call to deny oneself and take up a cross as even one part of a congregation's mission clarify what this call means and what it does not. For example, a cross is something we willingly take up for another, not something that is imposed on us by another. Preaching also helps church members understand that the congregation is a means of proclaiming the gospel and a temporary expression of the church, rather than an end in itself. Such preaching empowers the congregation to faithfully proclaim the gospel in word and deed, regardless of the consequences, because such proclamation supercedes the congregation's growth and survival, and even the congregation's existence. To follow Jesus is to give our congregation's life to God, trusting that God will bring life out of death, even the death of our congregation as we know it and, sometimes, even the death of the congregation itself. More than something Christians do for the church, Jesus's call to bear our cross is what congregations and the whole church do for the world.

Forgive and Be Reconciled

Drew looked down at the yellow pad on his lap. "Matthew and Mark might say that the risen Christ directs the church to teach and make disciples, but in Luke and John, Jesus's farewell instructions to the church concern forgiveness. Rather than telling the church what to do, the church is to tell the world what Jesus has done. In Luke, Jesus sends the disciples to witness that the Messiah suffered and rose from the dead on the third day and to proclaim repentance and forgiveness of sins in his name to all nations. John invites the church to live in the reality of what Jesus accomplished on the cross. Jesus authorizes and sends the disciples to forgive and retain sins. Paul says that Christ reconciled us for a ministry of reconciliation." Opening his Bible, Drew began to read, "In Christ God was reconciling the world to himself, not counting their trespasses against them, and entrusting the message of reconciliation to us."[3]

Christians and congregations that understand their mission as proclaiming forgiveness and reconciliation in Jesus's name believe that Christ's forgiveness makes community. No human community is possible without forgiveness. Without forgiveness, the community stops. As a community built on Christ's forgiveness, the church is a model for all communities, for the world, for peace. Timothy P. Jackson, who teaches Christian ethics at Emory University, defines forgiveness as the "cessation of againstness." According to Jackson, to forgive is to say, "It is with me as if you had never transgressed," which is how God forgives us.[4] To forgive people is to resolve to keep desiring and working for their good rather than to hate them and wish them ill, in spite of any hostility and wrongdoing that has gone on between you. Forgiveness involves giving up the hurt we legitimately feel and the justice and restitution we are rightfully owed. As Christian mission, forgiving others is one way Christians and congregations follow Jesus by denying themselves.

Some Christians and congregations proclaim Christ's forgiveness as unconditional, an act of pure grace. They point out that Jesus directs us to forgive people 77 times.[5] Other Christians and congregations critically assess how well people meet a range of requirements before they proclaim forgiveness to them. These Christians and congregations remind us that, in John, Jesus speaks of forgiving and *retaining* sins; if some sins are retained, forgiveness must not be automatic. In Luke, Jesus suggests that forgiveness is dependent upon repentance.[6] For some expressions of the church, repentance means that people must experience genuine sorrow and regret, confess their wrongdoing, and attempt to make things right. Brian noted that visitors, particularly people with little or no relationship to the church, frequently experience fear and coercion when the call to repentance is directed at them, especially when the preacher proclaims pure grace for those who claim to belong to Christ. For Brian, to embrace forgiveness as a mission means proclaiming God's unconditional grace to those who are coming to know Jesus, while calling those who have received God's grace and belong to the church to faithful living.

Congregations that understand their mission as proclaiming forgiveness in Jesus's name consider this forgiveness inseparable from the good news of the kingdom. Jesus's own mission included forgiving sins. He instructed his disciples to repeat the Lord's Prayer, in which we ask God to forgive us as we forgive others. Congregations that embrace forgiveness as their mission see themselves declaring God's love like Jesus and even participating in Christ's own ministry. These faith communities celebrate their reconciliation with and obedience to God by extending forgiveness and service to others.

To proclaim forgiveness in Christ's name as a congregational mission is to share God's gift of grace with no concern for how people will respond. Like the sower in Jesus's parable, the church scatters the seed of God's forgiveness with no regard for the condition of the soil. In this way, the church is like Jesus, who asked God to forgive those who crucified him as they were nailing him to the cross. Congregations that share in this dimension of the church's mission hope that forgiveness will make another feel accepted and bolster his or her self-esteem. They believe that forgiveness may induce repentance and contribute to people changing the way they live. They trust that forgiveness may bring some to faith and may even make them members of the congregation. Yet, these congregations are not motivated to forgive for any of these reasons. They know that, sometimes, Christian forgiveness does not accomplish anything in the person receiving forgiveness but only in the person doing the forgiving. In these circumstances, even when they occur among members of the church, forgiveness means allowing others to walk away and permitting broken relationships to remain until Christ restores them in the fullness of time.

While we often think of forgiveness as letting people off the hook, sometimes extending forgiveness involves holding people accountable. Even as we forgive, we cannot continue to tolerate attitudes and behaviors that blatantly contradict Christ, knowingly hurt others, and intentionally undermine the community. Sometimes, resisting these attitudes and behaviors leads Christians and congregations to end relationships. While reconciliation is always our goal, people may not be reconciled after forgiveness is given, as surely as they do not need to be reconciled before forgiveness can be extended. Expressing sorrow, naming sin, and attempting to restore right relationship are among the ways people internalize and respond to God's forgiveness. They are not stipulations for extending and receiving it. Perhaps this is why, in Luke, Jesus calls the disciples witnesses to what Christ has done, rather than charging them to do anything themselves.

Worship God

Pastor Mark explained that the church also uses Scripture passages other than the risen Christ's "farewell instructions" to understand its mission. Then Pastor Mark reminded the group of what Jesus commanded his followers to do on the night before he died. "According to Matthew, Mark, Luke, and Paul," Pastor Mark said, "Jesus told them to 'do this'—eat the bread and drink the cup, which Jesus called his body and blood, in remembrance of him."[7] The book of Acts attests that the members of the church "devoted themselves to the apostles' teaching and fellowship, to the breaking of bread and the prayers."[8] Paul declares that the church eating and drinking in Jesus's name is mission when he says, "For as often as you eat this bread and drink the cup, you proclaim the Lord's death until he comes."[9]

In and through their worship, congregations proclaim, to themselves and to the world, who they believe Jesus is, what it means to them to live a Christian life, what they understand the church to be, how they experience God relating to humanity, and what they believe is God's will and intention for the world. As I indicated in the section "Worship and Mission" in chapter 2 and when describing the sermon as a bridge in chapter 3, for some Christians and congregations, the most important thing God calls the church to do is to worship. For these congregations, the church's mission is to come together in Jesus's name to hear God's word and share the bread and cup, to baptize and to offer themselves and their prayers to God, and to give God thanks and praise. The Sunday service is the principal way these faith communities witness to the world. Going to church is something members do to witness to others, as well as a way they care for themselves. In and through its worship, the church makes disciples, takes up its cross, proclaims forgiveness, expresses love, points to the nearness of God's reign, and witnesses to Christ.

Preaching helps the congregation embrace and enhance its mission by proclaiming the gospel in such a way that the congregation contemplates how worship shapes and reflects its faith and life. Specifically, what does the congregation's worship communicate about Jesus, the church, Christian living, God's will for the world, and God's relationship with humanity? What is the connection between Sunday worship and God's will and work for justice and peace in the world? The preacher might muse that, while Jesus desires and establishes a deep and abiding relationship with us, sporadic worship attendance suggests that we regard God as a commodity we can use when we need it and ignore when we do not. Ministers standing at altars with their backs to the people surely communicate that the church believes God's relationship with humanity is such that people cannot approach God directly but need an advocate or intermediary to approach God on their behalf. The Lord's Table, where each receives a little and all have enough, is certainly a model of how God intends that we use the world's natural resources. As worship shapes belief and belief shapes worship, congregations both enhance their mission of praising God and deepen their witness to the world.

Love One Another

"Pastor, I notice that you didn't mention John's Gospel," Connie said with a smile. "There's no bread and cup in John's account of the Last Supper. Jesus's command involves a basin of water and a towel." Connie then recounted how Jesus washed the disciples' feet at the Last Supper. When Jesus finished and returned to the table, he gave the disciples a new commandment. Connie put on her glasses and read, "I give you a new commandment, that you love one another. Just as I have loved you, you also should love one another."[10] She commented, "With towel and basin, our master becomes our servant. Jesus shows us that loving one another as Christ loved us is more than a feeling and an attitude. To love others as Christ loves us means to humbly serve. Jesus teaches that real strength and growing in God's love do not come by power or authority. They come through acting in love for others. All Christians need to remember that we are to do what Jesus does for us. The most important thing preaching can do is make God's love as real as Jesus did, so our congregation will love one another. And people will know we're Christians by our love."

"Will they?" Lisa asked, "Or will they just think we're nice? We need to be clear, with ourselves and with others, that our actions are an extension of and response to the love we have received and that is ours in Christ Jesus. We need to make the link between loving service and Christian love so clear that people get the connection."

"But it's about foot washing rather than making disciples and growing churches," Eleanor chimed in. "I guess we didn't do a very good job of loving the Parson family." Over coffee the next day, Eleanor confided to a friend that she took great delight in pointing this out. But that evening with the preaching group, Eleanor was very serious. After almost 60 years of marriage and almost 80 years of church membership, Eleanor knows how hard it is to love others as Christ loves us, both inside and outside the church. Pulling a tattered sheet of paper out of her purse, Eleanor said to the group, "Someone gave me this a long time ago. I can't remember who. I've carried it around for years." Then, unfolding the paper, Eleanor declared, "This is what Paul says love is, without the fancy language." Eleanor read:

Without love, nothing counts—Nothing. And so we are to love. How? Be patient, be kind—even to people who are clearly in the wrong. Don't envy, don't boast, don't toot your own horn—ever. Don't be arrogant, don't be rude—even to people who really deserve to be knocked down a peg or two. Don't insist on your own way—ever. Don't be irritable—ever. Don't be resentful— ever. Don't rejoice in doing what's wrong—even a little wrong, even when rejoicing in doing something wrong is so fun. Bear all things—*all* things. Believe all things—even when to believe is to be gullible, even when to believe makes us stupid. Hope all things. Endure all things—all things, everything.[11]

"Either we take 1 Corinthians 13 seriously or we forget it," Eleanor said, "which means we cannot love others as Christ loves us without first being loved by Christ, and we will never fully accomplish this mission. And to love like Jesus means that we love without expecting to grow our church. Loving others as Christ loves us means nurturing others with no guarantee that our efforts will pay off, putting others' fulfillment ahead of our own, willingly making ourselves truly vulnerable, risking, and experiencing real loss."

"I chose loving one another, too," Fred said, "but I chose a different passage. When I read through the Gospels this week, it occurred to me that Jesus's command to love one another isn't really *new*. In Matthew and Mark, at least, Jesus says that the greatest commandment in the law is to 'love the Lord your God with all your heart, and with all your soul, and with all your mind, and with all your strength [and to] love your neighbor as yourself.'[12] Christ's love is more than something we do for one another; Christ's love extends beyond those who are members of this church. If we hadn't already spent time talking about Jesus's sermon in Nazareth, I would have brought that passage to make this point. I'm convinced that to love others, as Christ loves us, means bringing good news to the poor, releasing the captive, and freeing all who are oppressed. I kept reading in Luke and found other passages. In the Sermon on the Plain, Jesus describes what it means to love one another as he loves us. Jesus considers those who are poor, hungry, weeping, excluded, and defamed to be blessed; loving others as Christ loves us means treating people as Jesus regards them. In Matthew, Jesus says that whoever feeds, clothes, cares for, and visits the least of his brothers and sisters does it for him. In both Matthew and Luke, Jesus extends love to enemies and calls us to refrain from judging others.[13] Lisa was right when she said we need to be clear that our actions are an extension of and response to the love we have received and that is ours in Christ Jesus.

Seeking justice and helping those in need in and of themselves are not the gospel. But they are ways Christ would have us respond to the gospel."

In congregations that understand their mission as loving one another as Christ loved us, preaching is concerned, first and foremost, with Christ's love for us. Sermons certainly address Christ's love for individuals, the congregation, families, coworkers, those we go to school with, and all the other relationships and locations of people's daily lives. Sermons also proclaim the depth and breadth of Christ's love, which extends to people, places, and situations the congregation may never know but can come to care about because of Christ's love. Sermons lift up Christ's love for the physical as well as the spiritual dimensions of existence and Christ's passion for those who are most in need. They speak of Christ's love for all creation, as well as Christ's love for all humanity. Sermons proclaim the power of Christ's love to transform nations, institutions, and systems, as well as interpersonal and intrapersonal relationships. The proclamation of Christ's love cannot be minimized or presumed, or the call to love becomes an obligation, a burden, and an end in itself.

Sermons proclaim Christ as the source and power of love and not merely an example or a model of love, because Christlike love is not something we create, will, or conjure. We are dependent on God's love in Christ for both a rudimentary understanding of what it means to love and the ability to do so.[14] Our meager attempts at Christlike love result from Christ's love for us and for the world. Jesus can command us to love one another, and we can dare to undertake to keep this commandment only because we have an intimate relationship with God in Christ, which both models and empowers our loving relationship with one another. In fact, our loving relationship with God brings us into a loving relationship with ourselves and others. By loving God and others as we are loved by and in Christ, we become our best selves, the persons that God created us to be. We come to truly love who we are as we get beyond ourselves through loving and serving others, without first looking for personal gain or expecting reward. Once Christ's love is powerfully and vividly proclaimed, the preacher can call for loving behavior from the congregation, individually, corporately, and systemically, as a response to and participation in Christ's love for us.

Proclaim the Nearness of God's Reign

"I'm intrigued by the Gospel writers' description of both Jesus's mission and the mission of the disciples as proclaiming the nearness of the kingdom or reign of God in word and deed," Audrey said, finding her place in the Bible. "Matthew describes the beginning of Jesus's ministry by saying, 'From that time Jesus began to proclaim, "Repent, for the kingdom of heaven has come near."' Then, Jesus sends the disciples out with instructions to 'proclaim the good news, "The kingdom of heaven has come near." Cure the sick, raise the dead, cleanse the lepers, cast out demons.'[15] The kingdom of God isn't something the church does. God's reign is God's activity, which the church points to and announces and which people receive and enter."

The kingdom of God is a reality—an activity, the mission of God—rather than a place. Biblical scholar Marcus Borg argues that Jesus saw the kingdom as "God's passion, God's will, God's promise, God's intention for the earth, God's utopia—the blessed place, the ideal state of affairs."[16] Jesus's message about the kingdom of God, its coming and its nearness, is not about heaven. According to Professor Borg, in the Lord's Prayer, Jesus teaches disciples to pray, "Your kingdom come on earth." Jesus announces a transformed earth; Jesus makes known that God's love, justice, abundance, and peace is coming to earth.[17] The use of the word *kingdom* suggests that God will change the political and systemic realities of the world; the kingdom of heaven will be different from the kingdoms of earth. This is good news for the poor and bad news for the wealthy and powerful, because God's kingdom brings a great reversal of the way things are.

This approach to mission trusts that when people experience the dominion of heaven as near, they become disciples. The church does not have to *make* disciples. Therefore, rather than teaching people what they need to do, the church proclaims what God is doing and will do, inviting people to freely join in God's work in ways they find exciting. These congregations emphasize identity rather than membership, connection rather than participation, and community rather than institution. They are more concerned with the work of the dominion of God in the world than building or preserving the church. Their community is centered on kingdom rather than congregation. They are willing to risk that the institution may be lost as the reign of God comes near.

Preaching announces and points to this thing that God is doing and names the new reality that God is bringing into our world in the life, death, and resurrection of Jesus Christ. Sermons offer an image or a description of God's new reality. These images are often drawn from Jesus's parables. Throughout the Gospels, Jesus says, "The kingdom of heaven is like . . ." or "The dominion of heaven may be compared to. . . ." Like Jesus, preachers are not content with a single image, but use many as a way of recognizing that none completely hits the mark. More important, preachers use images that stretch the congregation and so help the hearers to experience the kingdom of heaven anew. The aim of sermons is that people experience God's world breaking into their world. They experience the nearness of God's reign. In this way, the sermon itself moves from talk about the dominion of heaven to something to which the kingdom of heaven might be compared.

In keeping with the preaching of Jesus, sermons call people to respond to and take part in God's kingdom. However, preachers only call for repentance after proclaiming a tangible experience of the nearness of God's reign. Then they provide the congregation with pointers on how to receive and enter into the kingdom. Sermons distinguish between life as we live it and the life that God intends and invite the congregation to live in the world as the world is seen through the eyes of Jesus. From this perspective, we also hear Scripture asking and providing answers to questions other than the ones we often ask. Rather than something the congregation does, the reign of God is the reality the congregation, and through the congregation the world, embraces by striving to live as if this reality is already fully present.

"All of these definitions of the church's mission are wonderful," Brian said. "They're biblical and holy and transforming. I'd love to be part of any of them, if I didn't have to worry about my job, paying bills, my kids, and whether I will have enough money for retirement. I guess I'm like the thorny soil I learned about in Sunday school." Looking over at Eleanor, Brian cleared his throat and recited: "'But the cares of the world, and the lure of wealth, and the desire for other things come in and choke the word, and it yields nothing.'[18] I still remember. We do the same thing here. We worry about making budget, getting volunteers, and that our attendance is slipping. People seem to spend lots of time thinking about the future. I wonder how preaching can help with that. Maybe next time we can talk about how preaching helps us face the future."

Questions for Discussion

- What do you understand to be the church's mission? How do you think your congregation defines its mission?
- How important are evangelism and the church's mission to your congregation? Why do you say this? How does your congregation feel about evangelism? Why do you suppose this is so?
- As you listen to sermons, what is the most important thing preaching calls your congregation to do? How do you experience that call—as an invitation, an opportunity, a summons, a command, or a threat?
- How do you measure whether your congregation is accomplishing its mission? How important are results to your congregation?

Chapter Eight

Can Preaching Help Us Face the Future?

"Maybe I'm the only one here who worries about making money, raising kids, and retirement," Brian teased. "I know I'm not the only one here who worries about the future of our church and our planet. Sometimes, I am obsessed with the future. I check the stock market to see how the economy is doing. I get all worked up about global warming and climate change. I'm afraid of terrorist attacks and want to do something to stop all the violence and war. I worry about what life is going to be like for my daughter. I wake up in the night thinking about my death. Then, I decide that I don't control the future, my own or anyone else's, and certainly not the world's, and so I just sort of give up. I really want to know how preaching can help me face the future."

"That depends on what we mean by *future*," Fred suggested. "Are we talking tomorrow, next week, next year, the end of our lives, or the end of the world?"

"The Christian church believes and teaches that time will end when Jesus comes again," Drew added.

"Yes," Fred continued, "but the New Testament describes Jesus's second coming in a variety of ways. Some passages focus on heaven; others describe Jesus's return to the earth. Some verses warn of judgment, and others assure us of God's salvation. Some passages depict God's future as a banquet with the Old Testament prophets or a marriage feast; others describe a paradise, garden, or fields of green pastures. Still others present God's future as a wonderful city with golden streets."[1]

Descriptions of Christ's second coming, the kingdom of God, or God's promised future include everything from unmediated access to God in the heavenly world to political, social, and economic liberation. Fortunately, God does not expect us to fit these images together like the pieces of a jigsaw puzzle. Though biblical renderings of God's future differ, they rarely contradict each other. Instead, these images represent ways that God's people have understood salvation at different times and during different circumstances in history.

"Who do you think controls the future?" Brian asked. "Who do you believe determines it? Does God alone control the future? Do God and humanity determine the future together? Or are our future and the world's future something that God leaves up to us?"

Believing that God completely controls the future leads some people to hope and trust in God's promise of wholeness and life, others to despair over displeasing God, while still others to fatalistically resign themselves to the notion that nothing they do really matters. "Vanity of vanities, says the Teacher, vanity of vanities! All is vanity."[2]

If God and humanity determine the future together, the future of both individuals and the world is an expression and a consequence of our relationship with God. Moses makes this point to Israel before the people cross the Jordan to take possession of the land that God promised. Moses' lengthy sermon might be summarized, "See, I am setting before you today a blessing and a curse: the blessing, if you obey the commandments of the LORD your God that I am commanding you today; and the curse, if you do not obey the commandments of the LORD your God, but turn from the way that I am commanding you today, to follow other gods that you have not known."[3] Some who hold this view attend to their relationship with God out of gratitude, as Moses suggests; others attend to their relationship with God out of fear. Some neglect or ignore their relationship with God altogether.

Others hold that God created humanity to be completely in charge of the world's future and point to God's intention, as it is recorded in Genesis. "Then God said, 'Let us make humankind in our image, according to our likeness; and let them have dominion over the fish of the sea, and over the birds of the air, and over the cattle, and over all the wild animals of the earth, and over every creeping thing that creeps upon the earth.'"[4] The belief that human beings are the masters of both their own and the world's destiny leads some to rejoice that they are in control, others to a deep sense of responsibility, and still others to abandon all hope because the future is in the hands of people like themselves.

"I'm confused about when God's future will come," Drew said. Then he asked the group, "Will God's future come at the end of time? Is God's future already here and breaking into our lives and the world right now?" Jesus indicates that both views are possible. On the one hand, Jesus warns, "You also must be ready, for the Son of Man is coming at an unexpected hour." Jesus seems to indicate that the kingdom of God is a future event. On the other hand, once when asked when the kingdom of God was coming, Jesus answered, "The kingdom of God is not coming with things that can be observed; nor will they say, 'Look, here it is!' or 'There it is!' For, in fact, the kingdom of God is among you."[5] For those who believe that God will bring God's promised future at the end of time, whether their time on earth or the end of the world, the Christian faith helps people to prepare for that moment. For those who hold that God brought or is bringing God's desired future now, Christianity is concerned with pointing out and receiving that future by living each day as God's people in this world, and trusting that, when we do live as God's people, tomorrow and the world to come will be but an extension of our ongoing relationship with God.

Even though both Scripture and our own reflection provide many possibilities for God's promised future, preaching about that future frequently is one of two kinds of sermons. The first type of sermon helps people to place their trust in God's goodness and promise; these sermons remind us that Scripture shows how God always brings life out of death and hope out of despair. The second kind of sermon uses the Bible to analyze statistical, societal, and historical data in order to predict the future, then tells people what they must do to be ready for what is coming. Sermons that call people to trust God's goodness and promise often approach the future in hope. Sermons concerned with data help people to watch and calculate the signs, often out of concern that people prepare for and secure their own future.

In this chapter I offer five ways of conceiving and preaching about the future. We might approach the future as (1) God's victory,

Figure 8.1. How Do You Understand the Future?

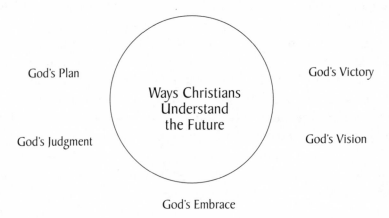

God's Plan

Ways Christians
Understand
the Future

God's Victory

God's Judgment

God's Vision

God's Embrace

(2) God's vision, (3) God's embrace, (4) God's judgment, and (5) God's plan. These perspectives on the future all suggest that the future belongs to God. While other views of the future certainly make for interesting conversation, including an understanding of the future in which God leaves the world and its inhabitants to their own devices, conceptions of the future like this have no place in Christian preaching because they are neither biblical nor in keeping with the gospel and are therefore beyond the scope of this conversation.

God's Victory

"Before we wander off into speculating about what God's future is and will be like, let's take a moment to recognize what an extraordinary thing it is to believe and say that God cares about what happens to us and to the world. Forget when and how. The future brings God's victory; God will triumph over all those things that are contrary to God." Pastor Mark raised an index finger and looked around at the group. "I believe that preaching the gospel gives us hope to face the future. The gospel assures us that the future is in God's hands. We know the end of the story. Jesus will come again and bring new life to us and to the world. While we don't know what the future holds, we know that God holds the future. If we don't say anything more, that's extraordinary good news. It's the reason we hope."

Jesus's life, death, and resurrection proclaim that God is present in every time and circumstance, bringing life out of death and newness out of seeming defeat. Old Testament scholar Walter Brueggemann observes that we often "fail to notice what a daring act of faith such an utterance is, how blatantly it speaks against and beyond perceived circumstances in order to 'reconstruct, replace, or redraw the threatened paradigm of meaning.'"[6] Only by faith can the preacher so powerfully speak and the members of the congregation so completely receive the assurance that God is not the prisoner of circumstance. Only by faith can the preacher and listeners hope that God can and will call into existence that which does not exist. Only by faith can both preacher and listeners anticipate what God is about to do. Faced with mounting evidence to the contrary, both in our lives and all around us, Christians and congregations sometimes find that the most difficult thing God calls us to do is to trust that God cares about and will triumph in the future. Yet, preachers often presume or assume that their congregations know, believe, and trust this extraordinary claim, and so they neglect to include it in their sermons.

Preaching about the future as God's victory lifts up what Christ will do and the good news that Christ has freed us from the power of those things contrary to God, including death and destruction, and that Christ is present with us in every circumstance of life. This preaching takes the psalmist's question to heart: "What are human beings that you are mindful of them, mortals that you care for them?" Sermons remind individuals that even the hairs of their heads are all counted. They assure communities that "all things work together for good for those who love God, who are called according to his purpose." Sermons that proclaim the future as God's victory assure the world that in Christ all things hold together.[7] For Christians, the good news that God loves the world so much that God gave the only Son, so that individuals and the world may have life in and through him, is the foundation for everything else the church may say about the future. The church therefore proclaims this foundational message about God's future explicitly and repeatedly. For some Christians, like Pastor Mark, everything else the church says about the future is an implication, explanation, illustration, or elaboration of the gospel.

God's Vision

"I'm not sure that I see any difference between sermons that help me face the future and sermons that help me connect my faith and daily life," Audrey said. "Both are about living into the nearness of God's reign and God's vision for our lives and for the world."

Christians like Audrey are not afraid of the future or unconcerned about tomorrow. Rather, they are deeply concerned with the future of this world and their lives in it. Paul tells us that the entire creation groans with the birth pangs of resurrection.[8] As these Christians consider Christ's second coming, they hope that Jesus will return and restore the universe to the life God intends. Their vision of resurrection is cosmic, corporate, and universal. The "new heaven" and "new earth" are the renewed or resurrected heaven and earth.[9] For these Christians, our future with God will be on earth where God will dwell with humanity forever. All creation will be in God's welcoming, unmediated presence. All nations and peoples will find a home in God's company.

In this vision of God's future, God will remove from the world everything that is contrary to God's will for creation, including fear, violence, domination, injustice, hatred, sickness, pain, mourning, crying, and death. Both Isaiah and Revelation present this vision. Isaiah declares, "And [God] will destroy on this mountain the shroud that is cast over all peoples, the sheet that is spread over all nations; he will swallow up death forever. Then the Lord GOD will wipe away the tears from all faces, and the disgrace of his people he will take away from all the earth." According to Revelation, the Lamb "will wipe every tear from their eyes. Death will be no more; mourning and crying and pain will be no more, for the first things have passed away."[10] For Christians like Audrey, this vision is not far removed from us by time and space. God inaugurated this vision in Jesus and continues to bring it into being through the church. God's vision offers us both a future hope and a present reality, which is breaking into our world.

God invites all creation to receive and enter into God's vision for our world, even as that vision is being realized, even as we wait for God's future to unfold and be fulfilled. Christians are to love and care for the world in anticipation of Christ's return. They are to love one another, care for their neighbors, and extend hospitality to strangers in a public and open way. In Luke's Gospel, Jesus teaches that God's vision includes preferential treatment for the poor over the rich, the hungry over the full, and the excluded over the respected; we embody God's vision through humility, hospitality, and acceptance of all.[11] Therefore, living into God's vision for the future also means repentance, turning from and eliminating all the ways both church and society treat people, institutions, and creation that are contrary to the gospel.

For people of faith like Audrey, worship embodies God's vision for the future and empowers the church, supported and directed by the Spirit, to work to make that vision a reality. For these hearers, preaching that is concerned with Jesus's second coming and individual preparedness must be balanced by preaching about justice and societal change. Regardless of whether sermons speak to the present or the future, these Christians want sermons that describe God's vision for peace, justice, wholeness, and healing, as well as individual and societal transformation in this world. They also want preaching that empowers Christians and the church to participate with God in making that vision a reality. In preaching, God empowers the congregation to participate in God's future as the preacher paints a clear picture of what God in Christ has done, will do, and even now is doing.

God's Embrace

"Dear, I think part of the reason you have so much trouble distinguishing between this life and eternal life is that you're so young and have so much life ahead of you," Eleanor gently responded to Audrey, who smiled to herself. It had been a long time since anyone called Audrey young. "Thank goodness, the world is going to outlive me," Eleanor continued. "If I have any future, it's in heaven, which I believe is another, better place. Jesus said, 'And I,

when I am lifted up from the earth, will draw all people to myself.'
I believe that Jesus drew me to him on the cross, and I take great
comfort in knowing that Jesus has gone to prepare a place for me,
and that nothing can separate me from his love."[12]

At some time all Christians distinguish between their own
and their loved ones' personal future, which they hope continues
beyond the end of this life, and the world's future, which will
continue until the end of time. In those moments, the promise of
resurrection becomes individual and personal. Christians often
contemplate the future as eternal life in heaven, an otherworldly
place beyond the moment of death where Jesus is. Christ calls this
place his "Father's house" and "paradise." Scripture also refers
to it as the "heavenly Jerusalem," our "eternal inheritance," and
a "better country." Whatever we call it, heaven is a place of the
everlasting blessedness of the righteous.[13] Those in heaven receive
life everlasting. Scripture describes them sitting down with Abraham, Isaac, and Jacob and resting in Abraham's bosom. They
reign with Christ and enjoy rest.[14] They are delivered forever from
all suffering and evil and eternally bask in the fullness of joy.

For those concerned with their personal stake in God's future, the church's mission is to help people prepare for the life to
come. Christians like Eleanor desire reassurance that God will be
merciful to them at the moment of death. They want sermons that
proclaim God's unconditional love and promise, which guarantee
their admission to heaven. These Christians welcome hearing that
Jesus died for their sins and will raise them to new life. They find
comfort in knowing that the faithful rest secure in the shelter of
God's wings; they are not overly concerned with details about
what eternal life will be like. These Christians simply want to
know that they are bound for heaven and that Jesus will welcome
them.

God's Judgment

"Eleanor, I think the reason you're so confident that Jesus is preparing a place for you is that you live such a faithful life. I wish I
could be so certain. When I hear that Jesus will come again," Drew

paused, "to judge the living and the dead, I can't help but think of hellfire and brimstone, weeping and gnashing of teeth. I need sermons that tell me what I have to do so that Jesus will judge me worthy of heaven and let me in."

The Gospels are filled with images of Jesus as our judge who will sort out the evil from the good, reward the righteous, and punish the wicked. Jesus tells parables in which he portrays himself as judge. Jesus is a farmer who, at the harvest, gathers the weeds out of his wheat and burns them; he is a fisher who keeps the good fish from a catch and throws away the bad.[15] Jesus is a delayed bridegroom who shuts the door to the marriage feast on foolish bridesmaids and a master who evaluates servants according to how they use the talents he gave them.[16] Perhaps most explicitly, Jesus compares himself to a shepherd who separates the sheep from the goats.[17] Jesus will invite the sheep to inherit the kingdom prepared for them from the foundation of the world and will send the goats from his presence into the eternal fire prepared for the devil and his angels.

The church fulfills its mission in worship and preaching by proclaiming what is necessary for entrance into God's future. Again, the Bible provides an abundance of criteria by which Jesus will judge individuals and the world. "For God so loved the world that he gave his only Son, so that everyone who believes in him may not perish but may have eternal life."[18] According to this verse, belief in Jesus is the criterion by which we will be judged. But what does it mean to believe in Jesus? Some regard Jesus's declaration "I am the way, and the truth, and the life. No one comes to the Father except through me"[19] as a tenet of faith, which people must ascribe to in order to be saved. For others, Jesus's declaration that he is the way, the truth, and the life implies a personal relationship; accepting Jesus as personal Lord and Savior guarantees access to heaven. For still others, "the way, the truth, and the life" is a description of who Jesus is and what he has accomplished, and faith is simple trust; nothing the individual does or does not do really matters. Those who hold that Jesus alone accomplishes salvation and that all we can do is trust in Jesus recall that Jesus said, "Truly I tell you, whoever does not receive the kingdom of God as a little child will never enter it."[20]

In other passages, belief in Jesus is to be accompanied by an outward expression of faith. In Mark's Gospel, the risen Christ tells the apostles, "The one who believes and is baptized will be saved; but the one who does not believe will be condemned." Paul tells the Romans that those who confess with their lips that Jesus is Lord and believe in their heart that God raised him from the dead will be saved.[21] In other passages, Jesus indicates that salvation depends less on what we believe and more on how we act. Jesus says that it is not enough to call him Lord; we must do the will of the Father in heaven. In other passages, Jesus indicates that we will be judged by how we treat the poor or keep the commandments. In one verse, Jesus even indicates that on the day of judgment we will be held accountable for every careless word we utter.[22]

Christians such as Drew who view the future as the day of judgment desire sermons that tell them and others what they must do to be saved. They sincerely find it difficult to accept that Jesus saved them or anyone else, regardless of who they are and how they live. We can all think of people who we have difficulty believing are saved. Christians who view the future as God's judgment appreciate absolute answers and clear instructions. These Christians want the church to take a stand and, like Jesus, to hold people accountable. Clarity and accountability help them prepare for the Christ who will come, whether on the day of judgment or at the end of their lives.

God's Plan

"I'm confused about the rapture," Connie blurted out. "Heaven is supposed to be a place where there are no tears or worry or sadness. I could never be happy in heaven if I was snatched away from my family into heaven and knew that my loved ones were suffering down on earth. How could God do that?"

Some Christians believe that God long ago planned both their future and the world's future and that God's plan is unfolding even now. History will end when Christ unleashes a seven-year period of global tribulation and terrible destruction upon the earth. These Christians often use the image of a countdown, as in a missile launch or a rocket blasting off into space, to describe God's pending destruction. "God has a clock that is counting down, its hands drawing ever closer to midnight. . . . God's prophetic stopwatch is ticking down to the end of the world."[23] For these Christians, God controls the end of the world. The countdown is underway, and nothing the world does will stop it.

As part of God's plan, Jesus will come and take or "rapture" Christians up to heaven before the destruction of the world. These Christians remind us that Jesus compared his second coming with the coming flood in the time of Noah. Jesus said, "For as in those days . . . they knew nothing until the flood came and swept them all away, so too will be the coming of the Son of Man. Then two will be in the field; one will be taken and one will be left. Two women will be grinding meal together; one will be taken and one will be left." In Luke's Gospel, two people who share the same bed will be separated as one is taken up and the other is left.[24]

Christians who look for God's coming destruction point to both 1 Thessalonians and Revelation as describing the end of the world and the rapture. According to these Christians, 1 Thessalonians says that Christians who are alive at the end of the world and left on earth will be caught up in the clouds to meet the Lord in the air and will be with the Lord forever. Christians who believe in the rapture tell us that Revelation invites those who dwell in the heavens to rejoice, while extending woe to the earth and the sea, as the devil comes down to earth with great wrath because he knows that his time is short.[25] These Christians interpret these passages differently as they look for precise details. For example, some think the rapture comes before the tribulation and some after—and some say it comes during the tribulation. Regardless of when it comes, the rapture provides those who believe in Christ with a means of escape from the destruction of the world and keeps Christians from despairing amid ever-worsening global conditions because only non-Christians will be left behind on earth. For those who anticipate a rapture, resurrection will be selective.

Jesus tells us to keep awake and be ready. Although we do not know on what day our Lord is coming, because the Son of Humanity is coming at an unexpected hour,[26] Christians who believe in the rapture hold that God provides us with a blueprint to follow so that we can discern when the end will come. God's plan for the end of history is mapped out in the Bible, they hold, particularly in the books of Daniel and Revelation. The church's mission with regard to the future is to decipher and follow God's roadmap in order to prepare people for the end.

For people eager to hear about Christ's return, worship centers around expository preaching on apocalyptic and prophetic texts. Preaching helps them to watch the signs and decipher the codes in order to determine the day and the hour, which, Scripture tells us, only the Father knows.[27] Preaching focuses on saving people out of the world. The goal is to tell as many people as possible about Christ, before it is too late. The urgency that Jesus taught about the coming kingdom of God gets translated into fear.

"So what have we learned from all this talk about preaching?" Fred asked the group. "We sure haven't resolved anything."

"But we're still talking," Connie said, smiling, "even though we will probably never agree on everything."

Like the people of St. Ambrose Church, your conversation about preaching has come to a close. Or has it? What, if anything, have you resolved? Do you still have more talking to do? In the epilogue, listen as the members of St. Ambrose Church reflect on their experience, which I hope helps your group to reflect on yours.

Questions for Discussion

- Which aspect of the future concerns you the most? Why?
- What is your vision of God's future?
- How would you describe the way God is involved in your future? In the world's future?
- How does the Bible help you face the future?

Epilogue

Reflect on Your Conversation

The most important lesson I learned from Christians who discuss the faith convictions they bring to the Sunday sermon is that neither I nor congregational study groups can predict how those conversations will impact a congregation's preaching, not to mention a congregation's worship, leadership, faith formation, common life, and mission. These kinds of predictions cannot be made before the conversation takes place, because God has not had a say. I have no doubt that discussing the faith convictions we bring to the Sunday sermon will be influential. I am certain that as you read this epilogue and reflect upon your group's experience, you would agree that God spoke to you in and through your conversation. But only you and your conversation partners know what God had to say. The book of Revelation indicates that God has particular messages for specific churches.[1] It is your joy and privilege, and perhaps your challenge, to discern together what God is saying to your congregation.

Groups in many congregations report that, as they listen for God to speak to them through sermons and conversations about preaching, they are helped in discovering what God is saying by knowing what others have heard. As I bring my participation in your conversation to a close, let's listen in as the members of St. Ambrose Church share some general conclusions about what they hear God saying to them in and through their conversation about preaching. Their comments reflect what many other congregations report they generally heard as well.

"So, what have we heard God saying to us in all this talk about preaching?" Fred asked the group. "We sure haven't resolved any of the questions we considered."

"But we're still talking," Connie said, smiling, "even though we will probably never agree on everything. I heard God saying that our congregation is stronger than the questions we ask and the issues we face."

"That we may never agree on everything might be a good thing, even a blessing," Audrey reflected. "My faith has grown. It's deepened and expanded because of these conversations."

"My faith is unsettled," Drew complained. "I'm asking questions and thinking about things I never have before."

Brian smiled approvingly. "Drew, I find it refreshing that someone like you, someone who is really faithful, can feel as unsettled as I do. Maybe God is telling me that I don't have to have everything figured out."

"I learned that I can't judge other people's faith by my understanding of mission." Lisa had wanted to say this for several weeks. "And that our congregation needs to do some serious talking and praying about what our mission is." Everyone groaned, then laughed.

"I learned that if we don't agree on what a sermon is," Eleanor said, "I shouldn't be surprised that we don't agree on other, more complicated things. But I can still be disappointed when we don't think and act the way I wish we would."

"God gave me a wake-up call," Pastor Mark added. "Since we don't agree on what a sermon is, I need to mix up my preaching in order to connect with more people."

"To help you do that," Fred responded, "we need to find ways to continue this conversation. We also need to have a conversation about how we read the Bible, because it seems to me that we do that differently as well."

These brief comments by the members of St. Ambrose Church summarize what groups in many congregations heard God saying as they talked about preaching. My comments on each of these messages, which follow, are a lot like postcards. They provide a brief snapshot of a message many congregations hear, but in no way do they capture the richness, color, texture, and depth that I trust characterized your conversation.

Our Congregation Is Diverse

Many Christians are genuinely surprised at how diverse their congregation truly is. They find that Christians and congregations are complex. Members' beliefs contradict one another; an individual Christian may hold beliefs that seem to be in opposition. Neither Christians nor congregations can be reduced to simple stereotypes or the sides they take on given issues. Once Christians and congregations recognize their diversity, they often experience the grace of recognizing that, as much as they might want to, God does not want them to ignore it, dismiss it as wrong, or pretend it is not there. Instead, God calls congregations to embrace their diversity. Of course, both Christians and congregations will sometimes identify perspectives they cannot or will not embrace. Paul might be able to "become all things to all people, that [he] might by all means save some."[2] Most Christians and congregations find that they cannot.

Through their conversations about preaching, Christians find that to name and share what they believe is both risky and rewarding. They gain confidence that, though it takes practice, members of a congregation can share their different beliefs and perspectives in ways that are not threatening. Many report that this kind of sharing deepens their faith and strengthens their church. Groups that discuss the convictions they bring to sermons slowly come to appreciate that tension is part of being Christian and being church and may even indicate the Spirit is blowing where it will.[3] These congregations find that members can hold different opinions, and even disagree, and things don't have to turn ugly. They learn that the faithful and healthy response to tension in a congregation is not to ignore or try to eliminate it. Rather, Christians struggle to trust God's presence and activity amid tension, so they can become comfortable enough with tension that it does not silence conversation or automatically lead to conflict. When silence or conflict occurs, Christians dare to talk about why this is happening rather than stop talking. That can be really hard. But sometimes God speaks a creative word most clearly amid chaos and conflict.

Listening for God to speak such a word, both in sermons and in conversation, takes time. Waiting patiently for God to bring new life through consensus, new understanding, or the unity in Christ that transcends a particular issue or conversation is hard work. God frequently speaks to us in ways we experience as tentative. Like the boy Samuel, we might miss what God is saying because we have not been taught how to listen. Or, like the prophet Elijah, who heard God in the sheer silence, we might miss the message because God speaks to us in a manner we do not expect.[4] Even when God speaks clearly, congregational response is often slow. Gideon tested God several times before responding to God's message; Ananias protested before responding.[5] God gave Peter both a vision and a message to extend the gospel to Gentiles; yet, according to Paul, Peter retreated from this message and withdrew from fellowship with Gentiles because of pressure from Jerusalem Christians.[6] Hearing, receiving, and accepting what God has to say can be as difficult for us as it was for our forebears. Christians therefore need to extend grace, forgiveness, and patience to both themselves and each other and sometimes even to God.

Preaching Is Leadership

Christians who discuss preaching regard the proclamation of the gospel as one way God powerfully leads the congregation. They also recognize that congregations and their leaders cannot take for granted the leadership God provides through preaching. Instead, preachers and other leaders need to identify how preaching can best function as leadership at critical moments in a congregation's life. For example, should sermons attempt to assert authority or to provide a vision? Most important, everyone in the congregation needs to be clear about the results they can and cannot expect preaching to accomplish. Preaching is less effective at getting people to immediately respond to a specific situation in a single, prescribed manner. Preaching is effective at shaping values, attitudes, and habits of behavior. Sermons can help people frame a problem, situation, or circumstance using the gospel; describe how the gospel informs and shapes our attitudes and actions; and identify all possible faithful responses so that the congregation can discern God's will together. This understanding of preaching as leadership suggests that when preachers and congregations assess results, they ought to look more to the long-term, cumulative effect of preaching than to the impact of individual sermons.

Congregations and pastors that discuss preaching also grow to appreciate what I call the "reverberating quality" of sermons. Sometimes sermons have their greatest impact days, weeks, months, and even years after they are preached as they reverberate in the heart and mind of a listener. A sermon might also exercise its greatest leadership when someone repeats the message to someone who did not hear the sermon. When the report becomes a testimony, a new sermon gets preached. The proclamation of the gospel moves from the pulpit into the world, and Christians exercise leadership that the preacher often cannot. As congregations experience the reverberating quality of sermons, they understand that Jesus calls all Christians to proclaim the gospel. Christians that discuss preaching make equipping and empowering everyone to become preachers (proclaimers of the gospel) a priority in their congregation's ministry, in their own lives, and in the lives of those they touch.

Everyone Participates in the Sunday Sermon

Groups that discuss preaching give up the notion that the Sunday sermon is something the preacher does and discover ways that everyone participates in making the sermon. They agree that preachers and congregations need to facilitate everyone's participation so that preaching can make its greatest contribution to Christian faith and congregational life. Preachers facilitate participation by transcending their own presuppositions and perspectives to cultivate more than one way of preaching. When preachers rely exclusively on one style of preaching or sermon model, regardless of what it is, they exclude some congregants from fully participating in preaching. Even in congregations that unanimously appreciate a single model of preaching, if such congregations truly exist, some Scripture passages and messages are best served by another approach.

Preachers might achieve greater diversity in their preaching using several approaches.[7] The preacher might prepare a single sermon (or a series of sermons) with one particular group of listeners in mind. The preacher might choose this approach when a particular group within the congregation needs a specific message. The rest of the congregation overhears the sermon and, when the congregation understands itself as the body of Christ rather than a gathering of individuals, rejoices that some members are receiving the particular message they need. Alternatively, the preacher may intentionally address more than one group within a single sermon. For example, the preacher might attempt to proclaim the gospel as both an answer and an experience in order to speak to both head and heart. As a third approach, the preacher might attempt to craft and deliver sermons designed for all the groups and perspectives present in the congregation over a season of preaching so that the entire congregation is addressed over the course of several Sundays. Of course, the preacher might develop the message and then consider how specific individuals within the congregation will hear it. Some of the best advice about preaching I ever received is to sit in a specific member's pew on Saturday afternoon or evening, read the sermon aloud, and consider how that member will hear it. By repeating this exercise in a different member's seat each week, preachers will become conscious of the different persons and perspectives present in their congregations and how best to preach to them.

Listeners report that they take their role in preaching seriously in several ways. They come to worship expecting to hear the gospel. They trust and anticipate that God will speak to and touch their lives through the sermon. When this does not happen, they might fill in missing pieces themselves. Amazingly, these listeners remain hopeful that next week they will receive what they need. Listeners explore what they can do to best hear the gospel from their preacher. This may involve changing their expectations or letting go of certain parts of sermons. For example, I deliberately check out during golf stories and lengthy, emotion-filled, first-person narratives. Listeners also pray for their preacher, for themselves, and for the congregation. They ask the Holy Spirit to center them and remove distractions so that they are fully present and open in worship. Most important, perhaps, listeners prepare themselves for the sermon by reading and reflecting on the Scriptures they will hear in worship.

Worship Forms as Well as Reflects Us

Inevitably, congregations that discuss preaching find themselves talking about worship. They come to appreciate that how they worship forms as well as reflects who they are as Christians and as a congregation. In and through their worship, congregations proclaim, to themselves and to the world, who they believe Jesus is, what it means to them to live a Christian life, what they understand the church to be, how they experience God relating to humanity, and what they believe is God's will and intention for the world. For congregations that recognize that worship forms them, identifying how worship shapes them individually and as a congregation becomes more important than defending personal preferences. Instead, these congregations discuss what their worship communicates about their beliefs and identity. They contemplate how they connect worship, preaching, and mission. These congregations find that considering elements of the worship service helps people step out of their comfort zone and results in a richer conversation.

We Read the Bible Differently

Even in the same congregation, people read and interpret Scripture many different ways. Christians can read the same passage and interpret it differently. For some, the Bible is history; every word is literally true. For others, the Bible is an answer book. Still others approach the narratives in the Bible as models of how God interacts with us and the world. Some Christians read Scripture for inspiration rather than for information. Others look to the Bible for a perspective or frame of reference on worship, the world, and Christian life. Still others read Scripture as a testimony to God's saving activity, a conversation partner, or even a conversation itself.

Regardless of how they read the Bible, all Christians agree that the Bible is God's word, that Scripture is meaningful and important for their lives, and that they take it very seriously. Christians are also clear that what they agree on about the Bible far exceeds that about which they disagree. From this perspective, Scripture unites more than it divides. In conversations about preaching, and everything else for that matter, we should strive to approach disagreements on how we read the Bible from this perspective.

Jesus Gives Many Approaches to Mission

Congregations that talk about preaching agree that God gives every Christian and congregation a way of sharing in Christ's mission. Jesus calls all Christians and congregations to participate in his work. The most important thing groups that discuss preaching discover about mission is that their congregation does not exist exclusively for them. The church exists for others; the church exists for the world. Those who discuss preaching are clear that sermons should do something. Somehow, preaching should make things different; it should make people's lives and the world better.

Congregations that discuss preaching also discover that Jesus generously gives us lots of ways to participate in his mission. They find themselves considering how they will and will not share in Jesus's work. They find that the shape and direction of their mission is determined, in part, by how they worship, the nature of the congregation, how they understand God's relationship to the world, and how they view the future. Finally, they find that identifying their mission is both more complicated and more time consuming than congregations, and particularly pastors, anticipate.

The Conversation Needs to Continue

After discussing preaching for a prescribed period, congregations often find that their conversation needs to continue for two important reasons. First, talking about preaching makes sermons better. The conversation itself revitalizes preaching. As preacher and congregation bring their assumptions, expectations, hopes, and needs out into the open, they increasingly make the sermon together. The gospel can then reach more powerfully and effectively into people's lives.

The conversation should also continue because God is not finished speaking. Our faithful God never wearies of bringing good news of love, life, and possibility. Preachers and members of the congregation can continue to ask, What is God saying to us? Discussing this question as it relates to preaching makes prayer an even bigger part of sermon preparation, both for the preacher and for the congregation. Asking what God is saying to the congregation also changes the preaching dynamic. Rather than the preacher discerning and delivering God's message for the congregation, the preacher and congregation listen together for God's message, and the preacher gives voice to what they hear.

Congregations and pastors are very creative in finding ways to continue their conversation about sermons and preaching. As I said in the introduction, they are also eager for models they can consider and adopt. Preachers and congregations that participate in the ACTS Doctor of Ministry in Preaching Program become experts at developing ways to collaborate in the preaching enterprise. Drawing on the work of these congregations and their preachers, particularly Doctor of Ministry professional papers and contributions from teachers of preaching, I will briefly describe three approaches to such collaboration: (1) reflections on sermon preparation, (2) input groups, and (3) feedback mechanisms.

Sharing Sermon Preparation

Preachers might review their sermon preparation routine with a group within the congregation, such as a mutual ministry committee, and solicit responses. Preachers share how they typically select and study Scripture, determine and craft the message, and deliver the sermon. Together, preachers and congregants can assess what they affirm and anything they might like to change. Most important, they can consider how the Holy Spirit works through the routine of sermon preparation and what, if anything, they might do to facilitate and enhance the Spirit's participation.

Establishing Input Groups

Some preachers study the passages of Scripture on which they will preach with a group of parishioners in order to benefit from their questions, insights, and perspectives. Members of the congregation participate in sermon preparation by reflecting on the readings and then meeting with the preacher. Some preachers create a special group; others use existing groups within the congregation. Some do not gather groups at all. They use e-mail or a chat room to discuss texts, ask questions, and gather insights with parishioners.

Participants might be asked how they feel as they read or hear the text, what mental picture comes to mind, what connections or associations they have with the text, what disturbs them about this passage, and what, if anything, is new. Sometimes, this group also crafts the prayers and selects the hymns for the worship service.

Some congregations and preachers seek input from specific groups. For example, they might attempt to strengthen the link between preaching and leadership by including the congregation's elected leaders, whether representatives or the entire group, in the sermon input team. These leaders might explicitly consider the relationship between preaching and ministry, then facilitate the possibilities that emerge from sermons. Alternatively, to discover what people outside the church are concerned about, congregations might ask new member classes or people on the margins of the parish to supply a list of texts and topics they would like to hear sermons about.

Some pastors read and discuss sermon texts as part of pastoral visitation. I always found discussing Scripture with homebound members very helpful. My exegetical training paled in comparison to their walk with God. Over time, when these homebound members trusted that I desired and respected their insights, they began discussing passages together over the telephone so that they would be ready to "help Pastor with his sermon" when I came to visit. Other preachers visit members at work. Some pastors meet members for lunch, at times with their coworkers. Others take a tour of the workplace and, when possible, shadow the parishioner and even lend a hand. The pastor might ask how the gospel influences the parishioner's work.

Creating Feedback Mechanisms

After engaging in conversations about preaching, both pastor and congregation might be ready to discuss specific sermons.[8] Parishioners should only be asked to provide feedback on sermons if the pastor and leaders are genuinely interested in what the members of the congregation have to say and if it is truly safe for people to answer truthfully.

The nature of the feedback parishioners offer often depends upon the questions they are asked. Asking people which Christian doctrine the sermon elucidated yields one kind of feedback. Asking parishioners how the sermon connected with their lives yields another kind of feedback. I like to ask, what, if any, good news did you hear in this sermon? And, what difference will this sermon make in your life in the coming week? I also ask questions aimed at gaining specific feedback. For example, if I am interested in preaching and mission, I might ask: after hearing this sermon, what do you think God is calling our congregation to do?

Some preachers seek feedback on and facilitate discussion of their sermons using, among other things, forums during the education hour and online chat groups. In some congregations, the focus of confirmation students' sermon reports has changed from summarizing the sermon's content to speculating about what God is promising the congregation and what God is asking the congregation to do in light of the sermon. This kind of speculation inevitably leads both preacher and congregation to seek out voices beyond the congregation in order to hear more clearly and fully what God is saying to them.

Preachers are sometimes least able to assess their preaching objectively, either because they cannot see the inadequacy of their preaching or because humility prevents them from claiming the profound impact their preaching has on the lives of their congregants. In such cases, the preacher and congregation might employ mechanisms in addition to direct conversation with the preacher, such as individual interviews conducted by someone other than the pastor, small groups, or a questionnaire or survey.

You have come to the end of one conversation and perhaps to the beginning of another. I hope that discussing the convictions people bring to the Sunday sermon has been an experience of holy and active listening for you. I hope that you heard God speaking through you. I pray that the church experiences preaching as holy and active listening to God, who in Christ speaks a creative, life-giving word and welcomes us into divine conversation.

Questions for Discussion

- How do you imagine the members of St. Ambrose Church you met? What do they look and sound like? Who is most like you? Who have you learned the most from? Who has challenged you the most?

- What surprised you most about the diversity of your congregation?

- Was there a time when your conversation got stalled or your group got stuck? Why do you think that happened? How did your group work through it? How might you have done things differently?

- Can you recall a sermon that reverberated through you to someone else? Describe how this happened.

- How do you personally prepare for the Sunday sermon?

- Are you interested in continuing to discuss sermons and preaching? How might this happen in your congregation?

- As you reflect upon this conversation, what might God be saying to you and to your congregation?

Notes

Preface

1. Craig A. Satterlee, *When God Speaks through Change: Preaching in Times of Congregational Transition* (Herndon, VA: Alban Institute, 2005).
2. Ibid., 67–86.
3. See, for example, Joseph R. Jeter Jr. and Ronald J. Allen, *One Gospel, Many Ears: Preaching for Different Listeners in the Congregation* (St. Louis: Chalice, 2002); James R. Nieman and Thomas G. Rogers, *Preaching to Every Pew: Cross-Cultural Strategies* (Minneapolis: Augsburg Fortress, 2001).
4. Acts 2:42.

Introduction

1. Roger E. Van Harn, *Preacher, Can You Hear Us Listening?* (Grand Rapids: Eerdmans, 2005), 29.
2. James F. White, *Protestant Worship: Traditions in Transition* (Louisville: Westminster John Knox, 1989), 18.
3. Eccles. 1:9.
4. Raymond E. Brown, *The Community of the Beloved Disciple: The Life, Loves, and Hates of an Individual Church in New Testament Times* (New York: Paulist Press, 1979), 162–63.
5. Acts 2:44.
6. Acts 11:3; 15:1-35, 39.
7. Jim Kitchens, *The Postmodern Parish: New Ministry for a New Era* (Herndon, VA: Alban Institute, 2003), 5.
8. Ronald J. Allen, "Foreword" in O. Wesley Allen Jr., *The Homiletic of All Believers: A Conversational Approach to Proclamation and Preaching* (Louisville: Westminster John Knox, 2005), vii.

9. Exodus 15:4-5.

10. J. G. Davies, ed., "The Liturgical Movement," in *Westminster Dictionary of Christian Worship* (Philadelphia: The Westminster Press, 1986), 307–14; Craig A. Satterlee, *Ambrose of Milan's Method of Mystagogical Preaching* (Collegeville: Liturgical Press, 2002), 312n13.

11. Margaret J. Wheatley, *Leadership and the New Science: Discovering Order in a Chaotic World* (San Francisco: Berrett-Koehler, 1992), 61, 66.

12. Ibid., 106–7.

13. Ronald A. Heifetz, *Leadership Without Easy Answers* (Cambridge, MA: Belknap Press, 1994), 22, 87.

14. Satterlee, *When God Speaks through Change*, 67–86.

15. Mary Alice Mulligan, Diane Turner-Sharazz, Dawn Ottoni Wilhelm, and Ronald J. Allen, *Believing in Preaching: What Listeners Hear in Sermons* (St. Louis: Chalice, 2005), 127–42, 144–48.

16. Lucy Atkinson Rose, *Sharing the Word: Preaching in the Roundtable Church* (Louisville: Westminster John Knox, 1997), 4.

Chapter 1

1. Ronald J. Allen, "Preaching as Mutual Critical Correlation through Conversation," in *The Purposes of Preaching*, ed. Jana Childers (St. Louis: Chalice, 2004), 10.

2. Jeter and Allen, *One Gospel, Many Ears*, 9–10.

3. 1 Cor. 1:18.

4. Heifetz, *Leadership Without Easy Answers*, 280n4.

5. Ibid., 20.

6. Matt. 4:25; 12:15; 13:2; Mark 2:13; 3:20; 4:1; 6:34; Luke 5:15; 8:35; 12:1.

7. Mark 11:18; Luke 22:2, 6.

8. Matt. 27:54; Mark 15:39; Luke 24:37.

9. In the following discussion, I am indebted to Hughes Oliphant Old, *The Reading and Preaching of the Scriptures in the Worship of the Christian Church: The Biblical Period* (Grand Rapids: Eerdmans, 1998), 1: 111–63.

10. Mark 1:14-15; 1:35-39.

11. See Mark 4:31-32.

12. Matt. 17:1-8. See Old, *Reading and Preaching of the Scriptures*, 137.

13. Luke 4:16-21.

14. Luke 4:22-23.

15. John 1:1-17.

16. Old, *Reading and Preaching of the Scriptures*, 137.

17. John 6:66; Luke 4:29.

18. Matt. 9:35–10:42; Mark 6:6-13; Luke 10:1-16; John 4:31-38.

19. Luke 2:41-52.

20. Matt. 24:3.

21. Mark 3:13-15; Luke 10:1-16.

22. Matt. 9:34-38; 10:7-16; Mark 6:7-11; John 4:31-38.

23. Luke 24:44-48.

24. Matt. 10:7-8; Mark 6:7, 13; Luke 9:1; 10:9.

25. Luke 10:16; cf. Matt. 10:40.

26. Matt. 28:19-20; Mark 16:20.

27. Mark 3:14; 6:30.

28. 1 Cor. 1:21.

29. Matt. 28:20; Mark 16:20.

30. Matt. 10:8, 20.

31. Matt. 10:32-33.

32. George Barna, *The Power of Vision: How You Can Capture and Apply God's Vision for Your Ministry* (Ventura, CA: Gospel Light, 1992), 28.

33. Matt. 20:25-28; cf. Mark 10:42-45; Luke 22:25-27.

34. Mark 1:14-15.

35. Luke 4:21.

36. Matt. 5:1-12.

37. Heifetz, *Leadership Without Easy Answers*, 22, 87.

38. Luke 15.

39. Luke 17:12-13; 18:35-38; 19:6.

40. John 6:15; 18:36.

41. Matt 16:22; Mark 8:32.

42. Heifetz, *Leadership Without Easy Answers*, 87.

43. Acts 2:41.

44. Allen, *Homiletic of All Believers*, 57.

45. Luke 10:1-16; cf. Matt. 9:35-38; 10:7-16; Mark 6:6-13; John 4:31-38.

46. Matt. 9:38.

47. 1 Cor. 3:6.

48. Heifetz, *Leadership Without Easy Answers*, 53, 20.

49. Ibid., 69.

50. Matt. 7:28-29; Mark 1:22.

51. Wheatley, *Leadership and the New Science*, 24, 72.

52. Mark 9:38-40; Luke 9:49-50.

53. Wheatley, *Leadership and the New Science*, 57.

54. Heifetz, *Leadership Without Easy Answers*, 20.

55. Old, *Reading and Preaching of the Scriptures*, 152–55.

56. John 17:8.

57. John 17:20-21.

58. Wheatley, *Leadership and the New Science*, 106–7.

59. Matt. 4:1-11.

60. Charles L. Campbell, *The Word Before the Powers: An Ethic of Preaching* (Louisville: Westminster John Knox, 2002), 73.

Chapter 2

1. Luke 4:16-22.

2. Vatican Council (Second: 1962–1965), *Constitution on the Sacred Liturgy: Second Vatican Council, Dec. 4, 1963* (Collegeville: Liturgical Press, 1963); *The United Methodist Book of Worship* (Nashville: United Methodist Publishing House, 1992) 33–50; Evangelical Lutheran Church in America, *The Use of the Means of Grace: A Statement on the Practice of Word and Sacraments* (Minneapolis: Augsburg Fortress, 1996), no. 34.

3. Old, *Reading and Preaching of the Scriptures*, 162.

4. Luke 24:13-35.

5. Mulligan et al., *Believing in Preaching*, 15.

6. See Satterlee, *Ambrose of Milan's Method*, 295–99; Craig A. Satterlee, *Presiding in the Assembly: A Worship Handbook* (Minneapolis: Augsburg Fortress, 2003), 49–50.

7. James F. White, *Roman Catholic Worship: Trent to Today* (New York: Paulist Press, 1995), 1.

8. White, *Protestant Worship*, 15–21; *Roman Catholic Worship*, 1–2.

9. Jeter and Allen, *One Gospel, Many Ears*, 21–48.

10. See Pss. 17:8; 38:1.

11. Lucy Lind Hogan, "Alpha, Omega, and Everything in Between," in Childers, *The Purposes of Preaching*, 67–82.

12. Satterlee, *When God Speaks through Change*, ix.

13. Thomas H. Schattauer, "Liturgical Assembly as Locus of Mission," in *Inside Out: Worship in an Age of Mission* (Minneapolis: Fortress, 1999), 2–3. Schattauer labels his three approaches outside, inside, and inside-out.

14. Luke 10:1, 17.

15. Luke 6:17-49.

16. Luke 14:15-24.

17. Rev. 22:1-2.

18. Craig A. Satterlee and Lester Ruth, *Creative Preaching on the Sacraments* (Nashville: Discipleship Resources, 2001), 17.

19. 1 Cor. 10:1-4; Rom. 6:4.

Chapter 3

1. Teresa L. Fry Brown, "The Action Potential of Preaching," in Childers, *The Purposes of Preaching*, 51.

2. Barbara Brown Taylor, *The Preaching Life* (Boston: Cowley, 1993), 32.

3. Childers, *The Purposes of Preaching*, ix.

4. Mark 11–12.

5. Rom. 3:28.

6. Mark 8:31-32.

7. Rose, *Sharing the Word*, 14.

8. Charles L. Campbell, "Resisting the Powers," in Childers, *The Purposes of Preaching*, 29.

9. Luke 23:43; John 11:43-44.

10. 1 Cor. 1:23-24.

11. Thomas G. Long, *The Witness of Preaching*, 2nd ed. (Louisville, KY: Westminster John Knox, 2005), 20.

12. Jana Childers, "Seeing Jesus: Preaching as Incarnational Act," in Childers, *The Purposes of Preaching*, 47.

13. Mary Donovan Turner, "Disrupting a Ruptured World," in Childers, *The Purposes of Preaching*, 135.

14. Matt. 6:1-18; Mark 12:41-44; Luke 18:1-14; 21:1-4; John 6:51-58; 13:12-17.

15. Satterlee and Ruth, *Creative Preaching on the Sacraments*, 36–38.

16. Anna Carter Florence, *Preaching as Testimony* (Louisville, KY: Westminster John Knox, 2007), 65.

17. Mark 13:11.

18. Florence, *Preaching as Testimony,* xx.

19. David J. Lose, *Confessing Jesus Christ: Preaching in a Postmodern World* (Grand Rapids: Eerdmans, 2003), 3; Florence, *Preaching as Testimony*, xiii.

20. Luke 10:17-18.

21. Florence, *Preaching as Testimony*, 63.

22. Ibid., xxvi.

23. Allen, "Preaching as Mutual Critical Correlation through Conversation," in Childers, *The Purposes of Preaching*, 1.

24. John 4:5-42; Matt. 15:21-28.

25. Allen, *Homiletic of All Believers*, 16.

26. Christine Smith, "Hospitality, De-Centering, Re-Membering, and Right Relations," in Childers, *The Purposes of Preaching*, 105.

27. Long, *Witness of Preaching*, 35.

28. Allen, *Homiletic of All Believers,* vii.

29. Ibid., 55–56.

Chapter 4

1. Matt. 6:24; 12:22-32; 21:23-27; 22:23-33.

2. Henry H. Mitchell, *Celebration and Experience in Preaching* (Nashville: Abingdon, 1990), 22.

3. Luke 7:38; Matt. 26:7; Mark 14; Luke 23:34.

4. Ronald J. Allen, *Hearing the Sermon: Relationship/Content/Feeling* (St. Louis: Chalice, 2004), 72.

5. Matt. 6:25.

6. James 2:26.

7. Matt. 25:31-46.

8. Acts 2:41-42.

9. Matt. 23:1-12; 2 Thess. 3:6-15; 2 Tim. 1:3-5.

10. Heb. 11:1-40; 12:1.

11. Taylor, *The Preaching Life*, 65.

12. Luke 4:17-20.

13. Col. 1:10-20.

14. John 15:12-17; Campbell, *Word Before the Powers*, 116.

15. Matt. 8:20; Luke 9:58.

Chapter 5

1. Thomas G. Long, "No News Is Bad News," in *What's the Matter with Preaching Today?* ed. Mike Graves (Louisville: Westminster John Knox, 2004), 148–49.

2. Ibid., 149.

3. Ibid., 150.

4. Matt. 19:16-17, 21.

5. John 3:16; 6:40.

6. Mark 16:16.

7. Matt. 10:22; Mark 13:13.

8. Rev. 21:1.

9. Isa. 25:6-8.

10. Martin E. Marty with Jonathan Moore, *Politics, Religion and the Common Good* (San Francisco: Jossey-Bass, 2000), 76.

11. Rom. 5:9.

12. Rom. 8:35; John 12:32.

13. Fry Brown, "The Action Potential of Preaching," in Childers, *The Purposes of Preaching*, 50.

14. Marty and Moore, *Politics, Religion and the Common Good*, 59.

15. Allen, *Homiletic of All Believers*, 28.

16. Marty and Moore, *Politics, Religion and the Common Good*, 31, 34.

17. Ibid., 86.

18. Schattauer, "Liturgical Assembly as Locus of Mission," in *Inside Out*, 16.

19. Marty and Moore, *Politics, Religion and the Common Good*, 33.

Chapter 6

1. Campbell, "Resisting the Powers," in Childers, *The Purposes of Preaching*, 24.

2. Ibid., 33–34.

3. See Matt. 12:50; 25:40; Mark 4:35-41; Luke 10:2; John 10:14-16; 15:5; 1 Cor. 12:27; Eph. 2:21; Rev. 19:7-8.

4. Gen. 12:1.
5. See Deut. 10:17-19.
6. Luke 14:23.
7. Ps. 18:2.
8. Heb. 13:8.
9. Isa. 6:1-8.
10. Luke 18:9-14.
11. Acts 2:6.
12. Matt. 12:50.
13. Luke 13:29.
14. Jeter and Allen, *One Gospel, Many Ears*, 3.
15. Heb. 10:24-25; 12:1.
16. Rev. 21:22.

Chapter 7

1. Matt. 28:18-20; Mark 16:15-16.
2. Matt. 16:24-25; cf. Mark 8:34-35; Luke 9:23-24.
3. Luke 24:46-47 (cf. Acts 1:8); John 20:21-23; 2 Cor. 5:18-19.
4. Timothy P. Jackson, *The Priority of Love: Christian Charity and Social Justice* (Princeton: Princeton University Press, 2002), 144.
5. Matt. 18:22.
6. Luke 17:3.
7. Matt. 26:26-28; Mark 14:22-24; Luke 22:17-20; 1 Cor. 11:23-25.
8. Acts 2:42.
9. 1 Cor. 11:26.
10. John 13:34; cf. 15:12.
11. Mark Mattes, "Preaching Helps: Fourth Sunday after the Epiphany," *Currents in Theology and Mission* 21, no. 5 (October 1994): 395.
12. Mark 12:30-31; cf. Matt. 22:37.
13. Matt. 25:31-46; Matt. 5:44; Luke 6:20-42.
14. 1 John 4:8; Jackson, *Priority of Love*, 8.
15. Matt. 4:17; 10:7-8.
16. Marcus Borg, *Jesus: Uncovering the Life, Teachings, and Relevance of a Religious Revolutionary* (San Francisco: HarperSanFrancisco, 2006), 252.
17. Ibid.
18. Mark 4:19.

Chapter 8

1.   Barbara R. Rossing, *The Rapture Exposed: The Message of Hope in the Book of Revelation* (Cambridge: Westview Press, 2004), 33.

2.   Eccles. 1:2.

3.   Deut. 11:26-28.

4.   Gen. 1:26.

5.   Luke 12:40; 17:20-21.

6.   Walter Brueggemann, *Cadences of Home: Preaching Among Exiles* (Louisville: Westminster John Knox, 1997), 19.

7.   Ps. 8:4; Matt. 10:30; Rom. 8:28; Col. 1:17.

8.   Rom. 8:22.

9.   Rev. 21:1.

10. Isa. 25:7-8; Rev. 21:4.

11. Luke 5:20-26; 14:7-24.

12. John 12:32; cf. John 14:2; Rom. 8:38-39.

13. Luke 23:43; John 14:2; 2 Cor. 12:4; Gal. 4:26; Heb. 9:15; 11:14, 16; 12:22; 1 Pet. 1:4; Rev. 2:7; 3:12.

14. Matt. 8:11; Luke 16:22; 2 Tim. 2:12.

15. Matt. 13:40-43; 13:47-50.

16. Matt. 25:1-30; Luke 11:19-27; Matt. 25:14-30.

17. Matt. 25:31-46.

18. John 3:16.

19. John 14:6.

20. Mark 10:15.

21. Mark 16:16; Rom. 10:9.

22. Matt. 7:21; 12:36; Luke 12:19-31; 18:20.

23. Rossing, *Rapture Exposed*, 2.

24. Matt. 24:38-41; cf. Luke 17:34-35.

25. 1 Thess. 4:17; Rev. 12:12.

26. Matt. 24:42-44.

27. Matt. 24:36.

Epilogue

1.   Rev. 2-3.

2.   1 Cor. 9:22.

3.   Cf. John 3:8.

4.   1 Sam. 3:1-10; 1 Kings 19:11-13.

5.   Judg. 6:17-22, 36-40; Acts 9:10-14.

6.   Acts 10:9-43; Gal. 2:11-13.

7.   Jeter and Allen, *One Gospel, Many Ears*, 15–19.

8.   Satterlee, *When God Speaks through Change*, 79–80.